Key Words
A Journal of Cultural Materialism

7
(2009)

edited by
Catherine Clay
Kristin Ewins
Claire Jowitt
Angela Kershaw
Dave Laing
Sean Matthews
Stan Smith
Vicki Whittaker

Key Words: A Journal of Cultural Materialism

Editors: Catherine Clay (Nottingham Trent University), Kristin Ewins (University of Oxford), Claire Jowitt (Nottingham Trent University), Angela Kershaw (University of Birmingham), Dave Laing (University of Liverpool), Sean Matthews (University of Nottingham), Stan Smith (Nottingham Trent University), Vicki Whittaker.

Guest Editor for this issue: Ben Harker (University of Salford).

Editorial Advisory Board: John Brannigan (University College Dublin), Peter Brooker (University of Sussex), Terry Eagleton (National University of Ireland Galway and Lancaster University), John Higgins (University of Cape Town), Andreas Huyssen (Columbia University, New York), John Lucas (Nottingham Trent University and Loughborough University), Peter Marks (University of Sydney), Jim McGuigan (Loughborough University), Andrew Milner (Monash University), Meaghan Morris (Lingnan University), Morag Shiach (Queen Mary, University of London), Dai Smith (Swansea University), Nick Stevenson (University of Nottingham), John Storey (University of Sunderland), Will Straw (McGill University), Jenny Bourne Taylor (University of Sussex), Jeff Wallace (University of Glamorgan), Imelda Whelehan (De Montfort University).

Contributions for prospective inclusion in *Key Words* should comply with the style notes printed on pp. 136–8 of this issue, and should be sent to Catherine Clay, School of Arts and Humanities, Nottingham Trent University, Clifton Campus, Nottingham NG11 8NS, United Kingdom (catherine.clay@ntu.ac.uk).
Books and other items for review should be sent to Stan Smith, School of Arts and Humanities, Nottingham Trent University, Clifton Campus, Nottingham, NG11 8NS, United Kingdom (stan.smith1@ntlworld.com).

Key Words is a publication of The Raymond Williams Society (website: **www.raymondwilliams.co.uk**).

Contributions copyright © The Raymond Williams Society 2009.

All rights reserved.

Cover design by Andrew Dawson.

Printed by Russell Press, Nottingham.
Distributed by Spokesman Books, Nottingham.

ISSN 1369-9725
ISBN 978-0-9531503-1-1

Contents

Editors' Preface	4
Guest Editor's Introduction: The Century's Wide Margin Ben Harker	6
Edward Carpenter 1844–1929: A Very Modern Victorian Sheila Rowbotham	8
On Not Forgetting 'the importance of everything else': Feminism, Modernism and *Time and Tide* (1920–1939) Catherine Clay	20
'Ours will be a dynamic contribution': The Struggle by Diasporic Artists for a Voice in British Theatre in the 1930s and 1940s Colin Chambers	38
Adapting to the Conjuncture: Walter Greenwood, History and *Love on the Dole* Ben Harker	55
'Ephemeral work': Louis MacNeice and the Moment of 'Pure Radio' Paul Long	73
'The better it is written the worse it is': Storm Jameson on Popular Fiction and the Political Novel Kristin Ewins	92
'Hard as the metal of my gun': Communism, Masculinity and John Cornford's Poetry of the Will Stan Smith	110
Reviews	128
Raymond Williams Foundation (RWF)	134
Call for Papers	135
Style Notes for Contributors	136

Editors' Preface

The larger part of the current issue, guest edited by Ben Harker, takes up Raymond Williams's observations on the way in which, in the first half of the twentieth century, a hegemonic British culture systematically marginalised those forms of cultural production and discourse which did not conform to its social and political orthodoxies. To complement this examination of 'the century's wide margin', we also publish two essays on authors and issues that were similarly marginalised, with Kristin Ewins's study of the interwar fiction of the novelist and campaigner Storm Jameson, and Stan Smith's unpicking of the poet John Cornford's complex relations with Communist orthodoxy, in the context of the Spanish Civil War which took him to an untimely grave.

With the present issue, two long-serving members depart and three new members, Catherine Clay, Kristin Ewins and Vicki Whittaker, join the editorial board, significantly altering the journal's age and gender profiles. Both Raymond Williams Society and *Key Words* owe an immense debt of gratitude for the dynamism and intellectual capital John Lucas has brought to both over the past few years, and particularly during their reconstruction since 2004. His most recent involvement has been, along with the Society's current treasurer, Jennifer Birkett, in finalising the arrangements for the notable left-wing press Spokesman Books to take over responsibility for the journal's distribution and marketing. Sean Matthews, past secretary of the Society and an incisive and energetic editor of the journal since the inception of its second series with issue 5, is departing to head the new Cultural Studies programme on the Malaysian campus of Nottingham University. We would like to thank him for his work and wish him every success in his new role. Both Sean and John remain members of the Society and will continue to participate in the journal as members of its editorial advisory board. The final production stages of the current issue have benefitted substantially from Jennifer Birkett's energy and hard work, and the editors would like to thank her for her unsparing attention both to detail and to the larger canvas.

Issue 10 of *Key Words* (2012) will address the lines of intellectual and cultural enquiry opened up by Raymond Williams's ground-breaking study *The Long Revolution*, on the fiftieth anniversary of its publication in 1961. While the issue will re-examine the arguments of the book itself, the primary emphasis, in keeping with Society policy, will be on contemporary work in the cultural materialist tradition it initiated. Submissions are now sought for this issue, to be with the editorial board by May 2011.

The present issue of *Key Words* is dedicated to the memory of Peter Widdowson (1942–2009). Peter's work owed much to that of Raymond

Editors' Preface

Williams, not least in the attention it gave to many previously marginalised authors and texts. His edited collection *Re-Reading English* had a profound influence on the composition of English Studies, while the journal *Literature and History* he co-founded in 1975 in effect named the project which was to govern his career as a teacher, critic, and educationalist. His later studies of Thomas Hardy, in particular, made a seminal contribution to materialist criticism.

Peter was an inspiring teacher, a natural scholar, model professional and steadfast socialist whose principled commitment, ready wit, and personal kindness won him many admirers and lasting friends. His work and example belong to a continuing history.

Guest Editor's Introduction: The Century's Wide Margin
Ben Harker

'If we are to break out of the non-historical fixity of *post*-modernism', Raymond Williams argued in his late lecture, 'When Was Modernism?' (1987), 'then we must search out and counterpose an alternative tradition taken from the neglected works left in the wide margin of the century'.[1] Issue 4 of *Key Words* addressed modernism and Williams's engagement with it; Issue 7 is concerned with that wide margin of neglected works. Our historical frame is British culture and society in the late nineteenth century and the first half of the twentieth, and the articles collected here are sequenced chronologically. Collectively they reflect the current energy of politically driven cultural history; written at a moment of economic and hegemonic crisis, to different degrees they seek the outlines of a better future in the resources of the past.

Some of the articles are directly committed to the excavation and analysis of marginalised culture, whether individual texts, cultural forms, institutions, or networks of cultural production. These belong to a formation of radical recovery research to which Williams contributed in essays such as 'The Welsh Industrial Novel' (1979). Others draw upon and extend an overlapping project, analysing the *processes* through which texts are marginalised and traditions selected, constructed, consolidated and renewed. Some of Williams's richest work addressed the hegemonic functions of constructed cultural traditions – what he called 'the use of the past to ratify the present' – and in turn explored the counter-hegemonic possibilities of historical work, 'the recovery of discarded areas, or the redress of selective and reductive interpretations'.[2] In this regard Williams's books, such as *Marxism and Literature* (1976), and essays, including 'Base and Superstructure in Marxist Cultural Theory' (1973) and 'Notes on Marxism in Britain Since 1945' (1977), stand behind and inform a number of the essays collected here.

Developing themes from her critically-acclaimed biography, *Edward Carpenter: A Life of Liberty and Love*,[3] Sheila Rowbotham's article gauges the late work and erratic afterlife of Carpenter. Situating Carpenter on the cusp of Victorian sensibilities and more modern ways of seeing, she traces his presence through the wide margin of the twentieth century into the contemporary scene. Here, she argues, his views on gender, sexuality and environmental issues enjoy a renewed resonance. Catherine Clay recovers and reconstructs the first two decades of *Time and Tide*, demonstrating how the journal showcased significant alternative writing traditions and formed a key context for the construction and articulation of interwar feminist identities. Her article makes the case for the journal's importance, but also identifies significant shifts within its priorities. Colin Chambers addresses the struggles through which the subject peoples of Britain's empire established a voice in British theatre, and pays particular attention to the overlap between these formations and the politics of a broader left. My essay explores how Walter Greenwood's novel *Love on the Dole* (1933) came to stand in for a body of working-class fiction of which it was originally only a part; in particular I recover the novel's significant but quickly forgotten mid-1930s adaptation for the stage, which I argue was central to the consolidation of the novel's reputation. Paul Long's essay is less an exercise in recovering a forgotten reputation than in defamiliarising a canonical one. He unsettles cultural hierarchies in re-evaluating Louis MacNeice's work for BBC radio.

I would like to thank all of the contributors for producing such illuminating articles, and to the professional and supportive editorial board of *Key Words* for the opportunity to publish this work in the journal.

Ben Harker
University of Salford

Notes

1. Raymond Williams, *Politics of Modernism: Against the New Conformists* (London: Verso, 1989), p. 35.
2. Raymond Williams, *Marxism and Literature* (Oxford: Oxford University Press, 1977), p. 116.
3. Sheila Rowbotham, *Edward Carpenter: A Life of Liberty and Love* (London and New York: Verso, 2008).

Edward Carpenter 1844–1929: A Very Modern Victorian
Sheila Rowbotham

Edward Carpenter was a supporter of many causes from gay liberation to workers' control, from recycling to vegetarianism, from rambling to nude bathing. His enthusiasms indicate how so much that was taken as 'modern' in the early twentieth century actually had been pioneered by the adventurous radicals of the late nineteenth century. Even aspects of our culture which we associate with the era following World War Two were being mooted by Carpenter and his pioneering Victorian friends, though the holistic connections have been lost.

He was in his late thirties when he sat down in a garden shed at Bradway, near Sheffield, and began to write his long prose poem *Towards Democracy*. He was trying to conceive a new 'millennium on earth – […] a time when men and women all over the earth shall ascend and enter into relation with their bodies – shall attain freedom and joy'.[1] Democracy for him was an inner state of being, a new way of relating one to another. Change, he believed must come from the force of human desire.

The publication of *Towards Democracy* in 1883 happened to coincide with a wider mood of social and political discontent. The Marxist Social Democratic Federation was formed along with clusters of small but fervent discussion groups in London. One of these started in October 1883 in the rooms of an idealistic young man called Edward Pease who was studying carpentry in the hope of becoming self-sufficient. It was called the Fellowship of the New Life, and attracted a diverse band of intellectuals searching for the 'higher life' through the creation of a 'communistic society'.[2] Early members included George Bernard Shaw and Havelock Ellis. Shaw and Pease would soon depart to form the Fabian Society, but later additions to the Fellowship would include Carpenter, the 'New Woman' novelist Olive Schreiner and the vegetarian and animal rights campaigner, Henry Salt. Members of the Fellowship of the New Life interacted with a wide spectrum of radicals who were convinced of the need for new kinds of personal relations as well as a more egalitarian society.

Though the emphasis they placed on inner and outer transformation varied, this enthusiastic utopian intelligentsia were convinced that fundamental change was on the agenda. Capitalism was lurching through the Great Depression, unemployment was mounting, social reconstruction through reform or revolution seemed imperative. As H.M. Hyndman, the founder of the Social Democratic Federation, had put it in his popularisation of Karl Marx, *England For All*: 'It is impossible to survey our modern society without at once seeing that there is something seriously amiss in the conditions of our everyday life.'[3]

They were, moreover, acutely conscious of being on the cutting edge. Giving their journals names like *To-day* and *Progress*, they looked with confidence towards a new future and assumed they would play key roles in its making.

Carpenter appealed both as a poet and as an exemplar. Writing in *To-day* in 1886, Edward Pease argued that poetry should be an act of exposition. Walt Whitman was the model, but he saw Edward Carpenter's *Towards Democracy* as in the same idiom: 'Every line of his work is modern, grandly modern.'[4] Early that year Carpenter had addressed the Fellowship of the New Life on the 'Simplification of Life', pointing out that anyone who did not 'want to be a vampire or a parasite', needed to find a less wasteful way of living.[5] He advised his audience of idealistic New Lifers to settle for one large vegetable stew, a woollen coat that could be recycled into the dog kennel and cutting up old hats into strips to nail creepers to the wall. It was to be out with the chintz and in with the sun, out with the lumber and clutter and in with the grace and beauty of use.

Henry Salt and his wife Kate were among those inspired by Carpenter's example, first at Bradway, and later in his market garden at Millthorpe. Salt left his job as a schoolmaster at Eton and went to live in a labourer's cottage at Tilford, in Surrey. He cut up his academic gown to fasten the creeping plants and utilised his top hat for shading a young vegetable marrow. Like Carpenter though, the Salts found country life too isolated, and trails of stimulating visitors would arrive keen to demolish the bucolic peace with arguments about the political and social problems of the day. Beatrice Potter and Sidney Webb, who were still courting, bicycled to Tilford in good spirits. A grumpy Shaw arrived soaking wet and proceeded to write his plays in the garden. Carpenter played Beethoven on the piano with Kate. Country cottages and doing your own cooking and washing up not only provided a means of avoiding the excessive cost of Victorian middle-class domestic households, they carried a certain alternative kudos. A strong puritanical strand persisted in the socialist movement; the new life was both anti-materialist and modern, while politics was to be about what you did personally as well as what you advocated.

Carpenter mixed a nineteenth-century faith in the evolution of society with the Protestant assertion of the need to make change personal. While he had inherited the Protestantism from his devout Scottish mother, his legacy from his father was very different. Charles Carpenter left his son not only a large private income from investments, but an interest in German Romanticism and Idealism as well as in American Transcendentalism. In his collection of essays, *Civilisation: Its Cause and Cure* (1889), Carpenter presented a critique of scientific 'objectivity' and argued that two parallel movements were at work in society. One sought 'a complex human Communism', the other was a 'nature-movement' which rejected machinery and saw salvation coming through 'sandals and sunbaths'.[6]

Romanticism inclined Carpenter towards a celebration of the body. His homosexuality meant that this was not simply a matter of contesting conventional morality but of defying the law. Inspired by Walt Whitman's vision of male comradeship while he was at Cambridge, Carpenter would later write with passion on the liberation of sexuality from the constraints and hypocrisy of the Victorian era and mount a courageous defence of same-sex love. Romanticism and Whitman also nurtured his interest in Eastern religion. A Cambridge friend, the Sri Lankan intellectual and reformer, Ponnambalam Arunachalam, encouraged him to read about Hindu ideas of spiritual enlightenment. In 1890, when Carpenter went to stay in Kurunegala with Arunachalam, he was introduced to a teacher who belonged to the saiva-siddhanta branch of Hindu religion, called Ramaswamy. The Gnani enabled him to realise another form of consciousness without thought, which he called 'cosmic consciousness'. Carpenter took away from his encounter with the Gnani two vital insights. Not only was the Western preoccupation with subduing nature through technology and science limited, but 'moderns' like himself were apt to be 'prey to the bat-winged phantoms' that 'flit through the corridors' of their own brains.[7]

As faith in conventional forms of Christianity floundered, the late nineteenth century saw the rise of several groupings inspired by Eastern religion and by Christian mysticism. The Theosophists, who embraced Eastern thought, exercised considerable influence, then there was a breakaway group of Esoteric Christians around Edward Maitland and Anna Kingsford who shared Carpenter's critique of Western science. Spiritual heterodoxies frequently overlapped with social and political ones, though not without a degree of friction. When Henry Salt formed the Humanitarian League with Carpenter's support in 1891, the anti-vivisectionist Maitland became involved. Salt, who found Maitland's monologues on the esoteric Christ during committee meetings exasperating, was aiming to establish a secular basis for ethics and inclined to Kant rather than mysticism. However the new grouping which concentrated on humanitarian issues and rights within civil society remained broad and eclectic in character. The League aimed to humanise the Poor Law, challenged the criminal justice system, exposed medical experiments on the poor in hospitals, tried to reform mental institutions and control the arms trade. It also opposed hunting, vivisection and all forms of cruelty to animals. It included many socialists, but it reached out beyond the organised left to a wide range of supporters of progressive causes. It established a terrain of ethical dissent around human liberties which would continue to affect the British left after the League itself disintegrated.

The second half of the 1890s was a testing time for both Carpenter's left-wing utopianism and for his sexual politics. Jingoism was in the air, the Independent Labour Party was struggling for votes and respectability, while the trial and sentencing of Oscar Wilde resulted in an atmosphere of panic around homosexuality. Carpenter responded with a renewed attempt to integrate the cultural and social aspects of socialist transformation. His collection *Forecasts of the Coming Century* (1897) included essays on literature, art, education, women's rights, as well as land colonies, trade unions and cooperatives. In his own contribution Carpenter proposed diverse 'Transitions to Freedom', by means of a combination of the state and various forms of voluntary collectivism such as cooperatives.[8]

In 1898, in *Angels' Wings*, he focused on the idea he had floated in *Civilisation: Its Cause and Cure* of a nature movement running counterpoint to the struggle for socialism. Carpenter's nature movement enabled him to incorporate an existential dimension of being, spirituality and psychological awareness into his vision of transformation. He argued that returning to nature was about celebrating life in the open-air of the countryside, paganism in religion and morals, orientalism in philosophy and a rediscovery of the primitive in oneself.[9] Moreover, Carpenter sought to dissolve the boundaries between art and life. Stressing that art should evoke feelings, he reflected, 'The Art of Life is to know that Life *is* Art that it is Expression'.[10] In *Angels' Wings*, Carpenter rejoices in flux, but he rejects art for art's sake, embracing instead the impetus towards art for all which was inspiring left-wing artists in Europe and the United States at the turn of the century.

How then did Carpenter fare in the new century? He was certainly not to everyone's taste. His close friend E.M. Forster recounts how Lytton Strachey, debunker of the Victorians *par excellence*, used to greet Carpenter's name 'with a series of little squeaks', while Vanessa Bell could not understand why Roger Fry revered Carpenter, who seemed to her simply a sentimental old Victorian.[11] Never the less, Carpenter could not be convincingly bundled away along with stuffy Victorian conservatism by the self-consciously modern avant-gardes of the new century. Instead he was able to reinvent himself, acquiring a reputation in many countries. In France his writings were appreciated by the group around Romain Rolland who wanted to connect art and life. His emphasis on simplification inspired the Belgian architect Henry Van de Velde, whose Weimar School was the precursor of Bauhaus modernism. He became a sage for American bohemians like the dancer Isadora Duncan, as well as for devotees of arts and crafts who hailed his work in their journal, *The Craftsman*. Far away in Japan, intellectuals and artists who were troubled by the impact of rapid industrialisation, read his work and searched for the simple life. Some formed alternative communities in the countryside; a settler at one of these,

Atarashiki Mura (New Village), who was called Nagashima Naoki, translated *Angels' Wings* into Japanese.

A questing schoolteacher in Leeds, A.R. Orage, who started the Leeds Arts Club and later edited the journal the *New Age*, played a crucial role as the conduit between Carpenter and an influential and self-consciously modern grouping of intellectuals. Orage was influenced by Theosophy, as well as by socialism, and pioneered the ideas of both Friedrich Nietzsche and Henri Bergson in Britain. He was preoccupied with reconciling the inner spirit of the individual with collective social change, and under his editorship the *New Age* not only explored the latest artistic and philosophic movements but debated anarcho-syndicalism and Guild Socialism. Carpenter wrote for the *New Age* and for another small avant-garde journal, *The Freewoman*, which also emphasised the Nietzschian will to change and refused to concentrate simply on the suffrage, covering controversial topics such as communal living and sexual freedom. Carpenter's writings on women's emancipation, especially *Love's Coming of Age*, as well as his support for the suffrage movement, brought him an enthusiastic constituency among modern women who wanted feminism to extend beyond political rights. Ironically, he would become for many young heterosexuals the guru of 'modern' democratic open marriages in which jealousy was expunged.

Less overtly, Carpenter's work on homosexuality and lesbianism, combined with his personal non-judgemental empathy, made him a significant figure among networks of homosexuals and lesbians, who corresponded with him about sexual feelings they were unable to express publicly. He struggled with issues which have emerged once again in the movement for gay liberation, putting forward ideas of both congenital and cultural homosexuality, speculating about a 'third sex' and proposing a propensity towards bisexuality among homosexuals and heterosexuals alike.

Carpenter, who was fluent in German and French, kept abreast of the latest scholarly publications and was in contact with the notable Berlin sex reformer Magnus Hirschfeld. A visit by Hirschfeld to London in 1913 led to the formation of a British organisation seeking more openness in the discussion of sexuality. Carpenter was a founder of the British Society for the Study of Sex Psychology (BSSSP), which included a group of men concerned to decriminalise homosexuality, supporters of birth control and early psycho-analysts.[12] The BSSSP could never achieve sufficient coherence to lobby for specific causes, though Carpenter did take part in a group which tried to promote sex education in schools. Nonetheless the Society crystallised the 'modern' resolve to understand sexual feelings pioneered by Carpenter and his friend Havelock Ellis. It also represented a marker in the long process of transposing same-sex love as one of several sexual choices into public discourse.

By the early twentieth century, Carpenter's questioning of materialism and a value-free science no longer appeared so heterodox. Not only was Theosophy attracting many adherents, interest in Eastern religions had spread from Hinduism and Buddhism to Taoism. Various forms of occultism also flourished, mooting expanded forms of consciousness, while the popularity enjoyed by spiritualism led to quests for other selves in other dimensions. At the same time new scientific discoveries were breaking down the old assumptions about matter. The physicist J.J. Thomson showed the energy within electrons; Sir Oliver Lodge suggested that electro-magnetic radiation pointed to a connection between matter and spirit. Even Carpenter's vitalistic Neo-Lamarckian views on evolution enjoyed a brief revival. Carpenter followed these new developments with enthusiasm. His conviction that the spiritual and the material were inextricably entwined spoke to the new era in which learned scientists could believe in ghosts.[13]

Equally his championing of outcasts and the marginalised was increasingly in vogue. In the early twentieth century, novelists, poets and visual artists were discovering the attraction of the open road and extolling the 'primitive' in other cultures. This was a familiar trope for Carpenter. From the late 1880s he had been inspired by Herman Melville's 1846 autobiographically-based novel, *Typee*, about the peoples of the Marquesas in the South Seas. Carpenter was also familiar with a work by the French anarchist anthropologist Elie Reclus, published by his friend Havelock Ellis in his 'Contemporary Science Series'. Reclus' book, *Primitive Folk: Studies in Comparative Ethnology* (1890), alerted Carpenter to customs by which gender was allocated culturally. Moreover, though Reclus retained some of the assumptions of evolutionary anthropology about 'primitive' peoples' childlike qualities, his anarchism enabled him to view other cultures with empathy.

Around World War One, Carpenter became increasingly fascinated by anthropology, producing *Intermediate Types Among Primitive Folk* in 1914 and then *Pagan and Christian Creeds: Their Origin and their Meaning* in 1920. The former enabled him to follow through his interest in differing cultural attitudes towards same-sex love, and both books explored Christian borrowings from paganism, a question which had interested him from his college days. Anthropology was just beginning to take shape as an academic discipline in the early years of the twentieth century and was still closely allied to the study of ancient history and the classics. Sir James Frazer's monumental volumes, *The Golden Bough*, exerted an influence which would prove particularly tenacious among artists and poets. Carpenter followed Frazer's approach of comparing customs across cultures; however his work also included some comments which suggest the relativism which was coming to the fore in Franz Boas' studies in the United States. Boas would encourage a questioning of the hierarchal assumptions about cultures implicit within the nineteenth-century evolutionary tradition.

Celebration of the primitive in the late nineteenth and early twentieth centuries was a home-grown phenomenon too. Irish nationalism fostered a revival in Celtic art and myth. This was paralleled within England by poetry and classical music which drew on a rural idiom, along with Cecil Sharp's earnest folk song collecting and Mary Neal's reinvention of folk dancing. Carpenter knew W.B. Yeats and his friend Florence Farr, as well as John Masefield and the musicians Rutland Boughton and Granville Bantock, all of whom elaborated on 'folk'. He was on good terms with Sharp and influenced Neal. The folk revival flowed into an interest in pagan customs. Indeed some of Carpenter's dissident Christian friends were starting to declare themselves as 'pagans'. Then there were the cheery young 'neo-pagans' at Cambridge, among them the daughters of Carpenter's friend Sydney Olivier. They camped on the wilder edge of Fabianism, wearing 'gypsy' scarves and delighting in sun and bathing. Virginia Woolf was pleasantly amazed by the insouciance of this slightly younger generation: 'Sunshine, nature, primitive art, cakes with sugar on the top, love, lust, paganism, general bawdiness.'[14] Some of the young neo-pagans had attended the progressive 'new' schools of the 1890s and would retain their enthusiasm for camping and bright colours into the 1920s. More sedately, Carpenter's friend Raymond Unwin created a rural urbanism at Letchworth Garden City, which sported a teetotal pub, a Food Reform Restaurant, a Simple Life Hotel for vegetarians, folk dancing and Jaeger woollen clothing. It also offered spiritual and political heterodoxies of all kinds.[15] Modified versions of Letchworth would be reinvented through other garden cities and the later council estates Unwin designed, all of which sought to bring the countryside into urban life.

While there are evident continuities between the dissident Victorian 'moderns' of the 1880s and 1890s and their early twentieth-century descendants, there are some significant differences which would become even more apparent after World War One. There was so much that the generation of the early 1900s could no longer take for granted: reality, representation, matter, spirituality, individual identity, art, Englishness were all being fiercely contested. With just about everything up in the air, moving as fast as you could seemed the only way to keep up. Connections which had been assumed in the past, now had to be juggled by theoretical prestidigitators. Carpenter remained open to many iconoclastic cultural shifts, but he was never quite *of* this era. He might be a sprightly rambler, but he had been formed by a very different mind-set.

Carpenter's socialism was infused by the interconnecting utopian vision of the early 1880s, when it had seemed that the new life would accompany social and economic justice. The material and the spiritual remained indissoluble in his outlook, as did the individual and the collective. Inner and outer consciousness, personal and public realms, work, art and everyday life were dynamically connected. When he started to talk about work, he went on seamlessly to hold forth on beauty in civic life; even as he imagined new sexual relations, he was conceiving a new community. Such organic links were not at all self-evident for the early twentieth-century 'moderns'. A.R. Orage, for example, had to labour mightily in order to bring together the individual and the collective in his political outlook. Abandoning the effort, in the early 1920s he would become a follower of the spiritual cult leader, Georgei Ivanovitch Gurdjieff, attracted by the promise of new forms of self-realisation through the collective in Gurdjieff's harsh system for breaking with old habits and ingrained responses.[16] It could be argued that many dedicated young recruits to the Communist Party would give themselves to an equally demanding, if secular and rationalistic collectivity.

Part of the problem in holding on to a theoretical integration of human activity arose not simply from an internalised fragmentation of perception but from the separations and demarcations inherent in the new kinds of scientific Taylorist organisation of work. Taylorism and large-scale production methods belied the hopes of William Morris' 1880s socialism of restoring craft and creativity to the worker. In response to Taylorism's attempts to increase productivity by breaking down skills, early twentieth-century anarcho-syndicalist and Guild Socialist rebels put the emphasis on the workplace as the main site of resistance. Other aspects of human experience, it was assumed, would change *after* workers regained control over their labour. This would have far-reaching consequences for other areas of left-wing activism because it accentuated the tendency within Marxism to make the industrial worker the key to social transformation. Areas such as consumption, reproduction, culture thus appeared as secondary. The emphasis on the producer tended to exclude many men; but it marginalised even more women. A young Canadian, Stella Browne, who had been associated with *The Freewoman* before the war and then became a key figure in the British Society for the Study of Sex Psychology, continued to struggle on the left in the post-war period, first in the Communist Party and then in the Labour Party, to overcome this divide. She argued that birth control was as essential to women's self-determination as workshop control was for men.[17] However her efforts to assert individual agency for women in relation to their bodies constructed a dualistic world of women and sexuality and men and work.

The fragmentation of the socialist vision became politically pronounced during the 1920s as the Labour Party sought popularity with the electorate and the Communist Party espoused a Leninist approach to strategy. It was never to be absolute of course; Carpenter's 'nature movement', along with Eastern spirituality, continued to linger around the left, though the rise of psychoanalysis meant that the 'bat-winged phantoms' were no longer being pursued simply by German philosophers, Eastern Gnanis, wacky Western mystics and sex psychologists, but by competing professionals with their own theories, journals and areas of expertise. The aspiration to live differently alarmed both Labour and the Communists, but the vegetarians, ramblers and simple lifers obstinately continued to regard the left as their natural habitat. The more extreme versions of alternative living might be contained in isolated anarchist communities or in eccentric communal experiments on the fringes of bohemia, but the idea of choosing how one lived entered the mainstream in the minimalist-influenced décor of small suburban villas which proliferated between the wars.

Carpenter's dream of art merging with life was only partially realised as interior designers watered down the twirling leaves of arts and crafts into mass-produced floral patterns for wallpaper. It was a bitter bathos. And meanwhile the fine artists and avant-garde 'modern' poets and novelists went off with subjective feelings and expression.

E.M. Forster feared that the reputation of his friend and mentor would fade quickly after Carpenter's death in 1929. Forster's own writings reiterated elements of Carpenter's desire for connection and new ways of being, though his explicitly homosexual novel, *Maurice* – directly inspired by Carpenter's life with his lover George Merrill – could not be published until 1972.[18] However in Forster's writing a shift is evident, the inward realm of personal relating becomes the source of subversion. It is no longer, as in Carpenter's endeavours, organically linked to a wider external transformation of capitalist society.

After World War Two, Carpenter's critique of a value-free science which in the late 1880s had seemed so heterodox, was more acceptable. It became recognised that social and cultural paradigms affected the framework of assumption. 'Objectivity' was no longer a given, but an area open to investigation. This would lead historians of science towards the fascinating connections between scientific concepts and mysticism which permeated the milieu in which Carpenter was writing. Interest in Eastern religion expanded and flourished, as did the questioning of the superiority of all aspects of Western culture which Carpenter had pioneered. However this critique would be accompanied by a greater awareness of the manner in which idealisations of the 'primitive' could represent yet another form of keeping the poor and the colonised in the place the Westerners had allocated for them.

The preoccupations of the Humanitarian League would take institutional root first in the League of Nations, and then in the United Nations' espousal of human rights. Campaigns around the rights of prisoners, mental patients and the disabled continued between the wars and would intensify from the 1960s. The National Council of Civil Liberties (NCCL), formed by an admirer of Carpenter's writings, Ronald Kidd, in 1934 to protect the unemployed hunger marchers, aptly elected E.M. Forster as its first president. After World War Two it went on to support the rights of travellers, immigrants and homosexuals, establishing the Gay Rights Committee in 1974.

In the second half of the twentieth century the emphasis on moral choice which had led Salt towards vegetarianism and animal rights merged with the social consequences of environmentalism to bring the whole issue of human beings' relation to nature to the fore. From the 1960s campaigners emphasised the dangers of assuming the natural world could be simply harnessed for human control. One consequence was that Salt and Carpenter's 'nature movement' began to move slowly up the agenda of social change.

Ideas of individuals exercising a choice in relation to how they expressed their sexual feelings, which had seemed so radical and extraordinary when presented by Carpenter in the late nineteenth century, would inspire both Gay Liberation and Women's Liberation. While gay men struggled to love without fear and contempt, women demanded the right to sexual pleasure without necessarily risking pregnancy. The challenge of non-procreative sex had profoundly radical implications which upset the hold of traditional religious assumptions. From the 1980s it would provoke a powerful rear guard action in opposition which sought to reassert familial values. However the self-conscious assertion of independent, individual identities continues to be evident in many aspects of contemporary culture. The extent to which it remains so controversial today is an indication of the remarkable radicalism of Carpenter and his pioneering circles over a hundred years ago.

However the pervasiveness and unpredictable manifestation of this notion of individual choice in relation to identity and lifestyle has not been a purely ideological matter. It has flourished within a form of capitalism which has relied on expanding consumption through a myriad of niche markets. The symbolic mystique of the brand has been pirated from radical badges and banners to convey, package, promote and sell aspirations for a better life. This has extended from goods to new kinds of service provision among those jostling for cash are innumerable healers and seers.[19] It remains to be seen how much will survive recession; nevertheless, we have many forms of individuality now on the market.

While the individual has now moved to centre stage, this shift has occurred in a very different context from Carpenter's holistic utopian vision of association. Indeed, one of our most difficult 'modern' dilemmas is how to *combine* individual expression and choice with new relations, not only with those we know and love personally, but also with those we do not know. When

Carpenter wrote *Towards Democracy* he roamed over vast terrains in fantasy. We, in our globalised world of virtual communication, ironically tend to see those we do not know as inherently dangerous and threatening. Hence we have the all-powerful individual beset by fear and divorced from the delights of human association. The anti-capitalist young seem implicitly to understand this, creating new forms of connecting community amidst protest.

The new circumstances of the twenty-first century make it possible to see Carpenter's ideas in a new light. G.K Searle observed in his volume in 'The New Oxford History of England' series, *A New England*, that Edward Carpenter as a 'fertile questioner of all established procedures and structures' deserved to be considered as a 'representative figure' of the period 1886 to 1918.[20] Carpenter was part of an influential radical intellectual milieu which consciously set about casting off the values of their times and their social class. Indeed, he was among the most vigorous trouncers of the Victorian age. In 1914, aged seventy, he declared it had been marked by 'commercialism' and by 'cant in religion, pure materialism in science, futility in social conventions, the worship of stocks and shares, the starving of the human heart, the denial of the human body and its needs, the huddling concealment of the body in clothes, the "impure hush" on matters of sex, class-division, contempt of manual labour, and the cruel barring of women from every natural and useful expression of their lives'.[21]

Despite the modernity of Carpenter's revolt, the vehement conviction with which he expressed it was actually most 'Victorian'. Taking him as a representative figure of his age involves a quizzical look at the one-dimensional picture he himself sketches for us. Recognising the many-sided complexity of a Victorianism which could produce such vigorous rebels questions the notion of an absolute antithesis between Victorianism and modernity. Carpenter's work and life also require a rethinking of the scope of 'modernity'. The kind of modernity he represents was politically and socially radical; he wanted a new culture in the widest sense of daily life, human relationships and a sense of harmony with nature, rather than simply a detached aestheticism. Carpenter and his dissident circle were modern Victorians and post-Victorian modernity would owe much to them.[22] Moreover his passionate recoil against the prevailing assumptions of his era propelled him into a remarkably far-reaching rebellion which remains surprisingly relevant today.

Notes

1 Edward Carpenter, *Towards Democracy* (1883; London: George Allen and Unwin, 1913), p. 5.
2 Fabian Society's Meetings Minutes, October 24, 1883, LSE.

3   H.M. Hyndman, *England for All: The Text Book of Democracy* (1881; Brighton: The Harvester Press 1973), p. 1.
4   Edward Pease, 'Towards Democracy: A Note on Edward Carpenter', *To-day* 6.9 (August 1886), p. 38.
5   Edward Carpenter, 'Simplification of Life', in Edward Carpenter, *England's Ideal* (1887; London: Swan Sonnenschein and Co., 1895), p. 95.
6   Edward Carpenter, *Civilisation: Its Cause and Cure* (1889; London: Swan Sonnenschein and Co, 1893), p. 49.
7   Edward Carpenter, *From Adam's Peak to Elephanta: Sketches in Ceylon and India* (1891; London: George Allen and Unwin, 1927), pp. 169–70.
8   Edward Carpenter, *Forecasts of the Coming Century* (1897; Manchester: The Labour Press, 1897), p. 188.
9   Edward Carpenter, *Angels' Wings* (1898; London: George Allen and Unwin, 1920), pp. 246–7.
10 Carpenter, *Angels' Wings*, p. 219.
11 E.M. Forster, 'Terminal Note', *Maurice* (London: Penguin Books, 1972), p. 218; Frances Spalding, *Roger Fry: Art and Life* (Berkeley and Los Angeles: University of California Press, 1980), p. 46.
12 Lesley Hall '"Disinterested Enthusiasm for Sexual Misconduct": The British Society for the Study of Sex Psychology, 1913–1917', *Journal of Contemporary History* 30.4 (October 1995), pp. 666–70.
13 See G.R. Searle, *A New England? Peace and War 1886–1918* (2004; Oxford: Clarendon Press, 2005), pp. 640–43.
14 Virginia Stephens (later Woolf) quoted in Nigel Jones, *Rupert Brooke, Life, Death and Myth* (London: Richard Cohen Books, 1999), p. 180.
15 Searle, *New England*, pp. 611–12.
16 See Alex Owen 'The "Religious Sense" in a Post-War Secular Age', in Ruth Harris and Lyndal Roper, eds, *The Art of Survival: Gender and History in Europe, 1450–2000* (Oxford: Oxford University Press, 2006), pp. 168–71.
17 See Sheila Rowbotham, *A New World for Women: Stella Browne: Socialist Feminist* (London: Pluto Press, 1977), p. 62.
18 On the links between Carpenter and Forster see Anthony David Brown, *A Consideration of Some Parallels in the Personal and Social Ideals of E.M. Forster and Edward Carpenter*, University of Warwick PhD, 1982 ; Paminder Kaur Bakshi, *Distant Desire: The Theme of Friendship in E.M. Forster's Fiction*, University of Warwick PhD 1992; Antony Copley, *A Spiritual Bloomsbury: Hinduism and Homosexuality in the Lives and Writing of Edward Carpenter, E.M. Forster, and Christopher Isherwood* (Oxford: Lexington Books, 2006).
19 I am grateful to Ursula Huws for this observation.
20 Searle, *New England*, p. 2.
21 Edward Carpenter, 'Reply to Congratulatory Letter', 1914 Appendix 1, *My Days and Dreams: Being Autobiographical Notes* (1916; London George Allen and Unwin), p. 321.
22 Jo-Ann Wallace uses the term 'early modernists'; Jo-Ann Wallace, 'The Case of Edith Ellis', in Hugh Stevens and Caroline Howlett, eds, *Modernist Sexualities* (Manchester: Manchester University Press, 2000), p. 33.

On Not Forgetting 'the importance of everything else': Feminism, Modernism and *Time and Tide* (1920–1939)
Catherine Clay

On 18 November 1933 the feminist and woman-run weekly periodical *Time and Tide* carried a review by the poet E.J. Scovell of a recent study of Wyndham Lewis, T.S. Eliot and James Joyce. The leading essay in the book in question (*Gog Magog*, by G.W. Stonier) bore the sub-title 'An Anatomy of Modernism in Literature'. Drawing attention to the wording of this phrase, specifically to the fact that it is 'not "An Anatomy of Modern Literature"', Scovell questioned the notion – already becoming a truism – that this canonised male trio represented 'the spirit of the age'. Casting the author as a kind of modern-day ghost-hunter, she warned: 'The danger is that the psychic sometimes exaggerates not the reality, but the importance of the thing he sees by second sight; or rather, he forgets the importance of everything else.'[1]

Scovell's challenge to the claim that modernism was the most important and representative movement in early twentieth-century literature strikes an important note in a periodical that – for the two decades under examination here – was consistent in publishing and reviewing the work of writers who contributed to the 'everything else' left out of modernist accounts. As will be seen in what follows, *Time and Tide* directs us to a number of alternative writing traditions that lived in critical and competitive dialogue with modernist writing in this period, and to a large number of neglected women writers in particular. While recent studies have brought more critical attention to writing 'beyond' or 'outside' modernism in these years, this article begins to chart the part that *Time and Tide* played in the mapping of early twentieth-century British literature, and argues for its own recovery in recuperative studies of the period.

My analysis builds on the work of critics including Ann Ardis and Gaye Tuchman who examine how in many ways modernism wipes out the earlier record.[2] But it also looks at modernism's influence in a more contemporaneous sense, through an analysis of the ways in which alternative women's writing traditions both claimed a position in British literary culture, and resisted their marginalisation during the very years of modernism's rise to cultural dominance and its institutionalisation in the university system. While it is not possible to provide more than an overview here of the writers and traditions that a study of *Time and Tide* brings to light, it is hoped that by demonstrating *Time and Tide*'s importance this article will provide some new directions for cultural recovery research still to be done.

The commentary that follows is structured with reference to the multiple and overlapping networks that comprised *Time and Tide*'s 'periodical community' at three distinct phases in the journal's development.[3] First, I consider the importance of suffrage, socialist and professional women's networks for the construction of *Time and Tide*'s feminist political and modern identity in post-war periodical culture (1920–1927). Second, I examine *Time and Tide*'s 'literary turn' in and after 1928, and the widening networks of modern women writers the journal drew upon to establish its position within the periodical marketplace (1928–1935). Third, I identify in *Time and Tide*'s 'sociological turn' in October 1935 a broad alignment with the politicisation of art and literature in the 1930s that also keeps open a dialogue on the relationship between politics and literature and the function of the literary artist (1935–1939). Throughout I argue that *Time and Tide*'s periodical community remained hugely important for women writers during the interwar years and, as the only female-run periodical of its kind, retained a unique identity in British periodical culture.

'The Modern Weekly for the Modern Woman': *Time and Tide*'s Feminist Identity (1920–1927)

During its early years none of *Time and Tide*'s contributors were writers we have come to think of as 'modernist', with the exception of Rebecca West, who wrote weekly theatre criticisms until August 1921 and joined the paper's Board of Directors in 1922. Among those listed in the contents bill of the first issue (14 May 1920) were the poet Alice Meynell, and the novelist and playwright Elizabeth Robins, both representative of a pre-war generation lambasted in the modernist project of 'making it new'. Importantly, both were leading literary figures in the women's suffrage movement (as, of course, was West) which provided by far the largest base for *Time and Tide*'s contributors in the early years. Other key contributors drawn from suffrage networks include Cicely Hamilton, a director from 1921 who wrote regularly for *Time and Tide* for more than two decades, and Christopher St John (Christabel Marshall) who contributed weekly music criticisms for nearly ten years as well as theatre criticisms, book reviews and later Gramophone Notes. A significant amount of creative work published in *Time and Tide* in the early 1920s was also drawn from suffrage networks. Helen Cruickshank, Beatrice Harraden, Helen Friedlaender, Louisa I. Lumsden, Cynthia Maguire, 'Susan Miles', Mary Richardson, Grace Tollemache, Vera Wentworth, E. Ayrton Zangwill all contributed poems and/or short fiction in this period, as did such male supporters of women's suffrage as Laurence Housman and Gerald Gould.

These and other suffrage signatures played an important part in the construction of *Time and Tide*'s early feminist identity and foreground a tradition of political and educational writing that was a hallmark of suffrage literature.[4] Many of these writers were members of the Women Writers Suffrage League, an organisation that 'sought to harness literary activity to political and social change'.[5] While the suffrage struggle had been substantially won in the (partial) extension of the franchise to women in 1918, for writers associated with *Time and Tide* the work of politicising and educating readers in feminist print culture was ongoing. In this period *Time and Tide* shared a number of features with suffrage journalism, for example, its regular 'Personalities and Powers' which used a staple suffrage genre, the biographical sketch, to 'discuss […] women as well as men of achievement'.[6] The frequency of the suffrage signature in these years illustrates the importance *Time and Tide* attached to the pre-war feminist generation and its political and aesthetic practices. In contrast with modernism's emphatic break with the past, *Time and Tide* stressed continuity with writers who, as one contributor wrote in November 1920, 'form[s] a link between the days of the past and the present day'.[7]

A second constitutive network in this early period was that of Labour and socialist women. In its first issue *Time and Tide* published a verse-drama by the Independent Labour Party member Margaret MacNamara; in subsequent years *Time and Tide* published pieces by Leonora Eyles (editor and contributor to the women's pages of the *Daily Herald* and *Labour Leader*), including, in serial form, her study of working-class women's lives *The Woman in the Little House* (1922). The most significant socialist women writers for *Time and Tide*, however, were the poet and children's writer Eleanor Farjeon, and the novelist, journalist, biographer and future Labour MP Mary Agnes Hamilton.[8] Farjeon was a regular writer in the 1920s for the socialist *Daily Herald*, to which she contributed verse-satires on the news in the guise of 'Tomfool'.[9] From May 1922 she contributed a similar feature to *Time and Tide*, a weekly round-up of the news in verse published under the pseudonym 'Chimaera'. It is quite likely that it was Farjeon who introduced other left-wing contributors of poetry to *Time and Tide*; poems by James Guthrie (artist and leading figure in the small press movement) and Margaret Maitland Radford (daughter of the radical *fin-de-siècle* poet Dollie Radford) were published in *Time and Tide* from late 1922 to 1926. Hamilton, a suffragist, socialist and pacifist who also worked on the staff of *The Economist*, reviewed books for *Time and Tide* for more than a decade and infused the periodical's book columns with overtly political criticism.

Perhaps more than any other part of the paper, *Time and Tide*'s book review section reveals what Jason Harding describes as an 'ongoing cultural conversation' that can be heard in periodical texts, 'a dialogue with a shifting set of interlocking periodical structures and networks'.[10] A close friend of

Lady Rhondda, Hamilton was also well acquainted with Virginia Woolf and the Bloomsbury group, and her reviews for *Time and Tide* reflect the tension between art and politics in literary debates at this time. This is Hamilton writing in November 1920:

> Politics overshadows the whole of our horizon. To tell the artist, in whatever medium he works, to leave them alone is ridiculous. The fact may have disastrous artistic reactions, but there it is. In so far as the novelist, in particular, is attempting to render the strange, irregular rhythm of life – of contemporary life – he must write about politics.[11]

Here the language Hamilton uses to define the artistic concerns of the novelist is quite modernistic ('strange', 'irregular rhythm', 'contemporary life'); at the same time she firmly rebuts the modernist view that art should rise above politics. An author herself of novels with overt political themes, she returned again and again to the subject of political fiction and refused to see these terms as mutually exclusive:

> I make no apology for putting together three pamphlets on Unemployment and two novels. When we see that the substance of fiction, and the substance of politics and economics are one and the same thing, then, and not till then, we shall have good novels, 'clean,' and above all intelligent politics, and sound economics.[12]

Hamilton's insistence on the inseparability of art and politics in her evaluation of 'good novels' engages with important questions about literary value that, by the mid-1920s, were already being answered in favour of a 'high' modernist aesthetic that successfully eliminated writers like Hamilton from the historical record. To recover this writing in *Time and Tide* is in itself to recover another alternative discourse or engagement with modernism, and to demonstrate the central role that this periodical played in mediating culture and influencing cultural debate beyond the narrow horizons of 'little magazines'.

At the same time, in the context of the literature/journalism divide that moved to the foreground during this period, identification with journalism has played a significant part in the historical amnesia surrounding the work of many women writers who contributed to *Time and Tide*.[13] Many of the periodical's regular writers sustained a prolific journalistic output throughout their professional writing careers. Among them were the novelist and playwright Clemence Dane (who later became Life President of the Society of Women Journalists), who was commissioned by *Time and Tide* for light features in the early years. The novelists Rose Macaulay and Naomi Royde-Smith, and the poet Sylvia Lynd, all made a living from journalism and were among *Time and Tide*'s early reviewers of new novels. Vera Brittain and Winifred Holtby, who moved to London together in 1922 to pursue careers in literature and journalism, had some of their earliest journalistic writing published in *Time and Tide*. Despite their positioning on the 'wrong' side of the literature/journalism divide, however, these writers do not treat journalism with the kind of disdain that is characteristic of their modernist contemporaries.[14] As Patrick Collier notes, 'the historical openness of the profession of journalism to women' and 'the central role journalism played in the suffrage movement' gave women writers cause to define journalism in more positive terms than was customary in a wider narrative of journalistic decline in this period.[15] Also crucial here is journalism's relationship to what Alice Staveley describes as 'women's fiscal modernity' defined through 'women's aspirations for a professional identity'.[16] Women writers like Holtby embraced their journalistic identity and the world of professional work it opened to them. Indeed, at a time of an unprecedented opening up of the professions to women, journalism itself became a vehicle for publicising the world of women's work and educating readers on the subject of professional opportunities for women.

Time and Tide's early feminist identity was centrally bound up with its construction of the modern woman as professional worker, and underlines the importance that Lucy Delap and Maria DiCenzo attach to 'distinguishing and disengaging the often implied concept of modernity from modernism', in order to put back into the frame the full range of feminist operations in political, intellectual and cultural spheres.[17] In early advertisements *Time and Tide* was billed as 'The Modern Weekly for the Modern Woman', fashioning itself as a periodical for an emergent class of professional women that was seen as distinctively 'new'.[18] Repeatedly in its pages *Time and Tide* publicised the woman as professional worker, from leading articles on such issues as equal pay and the marriage bar, to biographical sketches of women who had succeeded in professions traditionally occupied by men. In October and November 1926 Lady Rhondda (writing as 'Candida') contributed a series of articles on 'Women of the Leisured Classes' whom she regarded as a danger to society, echoing Olive Schreiner's discussion of 'sex-parasitism' in *Woman and Labour* (1911).[19] The announcement of a new feature from October 1920 further illustrates *Time and Tide*'s focus on the woman worker in these years:

> It is proposed in 'The Minute Hand' to deal with the minor events of the hour. We shall endeavour to give especial notice to the ebb and flow of the tide which, in its advance, opens new opportunities of service and achievement to those hitherto excluded. In the past, opportunities in Parliament, in public office, in education, in business, have opened in turn

to Jews, to Roman Catholics, and to working-men. To-day they are opening to women. So, in our watch of this tide, we shall be concerned very largely with this specially characteristic feature of our times.[20]

This editorial commentary demonstrates that, like other feminist periodicals of the early twentieth century, *Time and Tide* was far more interested in 'innovative ideas and attitudes' than in formal literary experiments.[21] By singling out the opening up of Parliament, public office and the professions to women as a 'specially characteristic feature of our times' *Time and Tide* underlines its deep engagement with women's relationship to modernity. At the same time, its insistence on the passage of time with its watch of 'the ebb and flow of the tide' also carries suggestive echoes of a central modernist motif that foregrounds the ways in which the languages of modernity and modernism intertwine in this periodical text. Indeed, these echoes gather pace on the back of two other minor features that also used the title of the periodical as a guiding metaphor. These were 'In the Tideway', a weekly column dating from 4 June 1920 that maintained a vigilant eye on the representation of women in the news, and 'Time Table', a calendar of forthcoming political and cultural events dating from 9 July 1920. But they reverberate even more strongly in the light of the central image emblazoned in the journal's title banner. Here the familiar face of Big Ben towers above the Thames, an emblem of chronological time poised with the cyclical rhythms of natural forces. A visual metaphor for women's relationship to modernity, its meanings ripple outwards: the arrival of women as voters and Members of Parliament, turning the tide of opinion on women's role in public and political life, a 'celebration of progress' that Delap and DiCenzo observe to characterise feminist writing in this period in contrast with an 'anti-modern politics' in modernist responses to new mass media and democracy.[22] At once registering modernist discourses, and resisting their hegemonic power, *Time and Tide* constructed its modern feminist identity in 1920s periodical culture.

Shifting the lens from modernism to modernity thus enables us to read *Time and Tide*'s development of a differently inflected cultural discourse, one that will prove more receptive to the writings and achievements of women. Significantly, *Time and Tide* did review the work of the female modernists Dorothy Richardson and Virginia Woolf, but it was absolutely silent on modernism's two 'landmark' texts of 1922, *The Waste Land* and *Ulysses*. In effect, *Time and Tide* simply wasn't looking at the canonised trio of Lewis, Eliot and Joyce in these years, but this does not mean that the writers it was looking at were unimportant. Indeed, in its 'watch of this tide' *Time and Tide* reviewed and published many of the most popular and critically neglected women writers of this decade, including Rose Allatini, Iris Barry, Stella Benson, Richmal Crompton, E.M. Delafield,

Susan Ertz, Eleanor Farjeon, Susan Glaspell, Winifred Holtby, Ethel Mannin, Viola Meynell, Hilda Reid, Sylvia Thompson, Sylvia Townsend Warner and E.H. Young. All of these writers had one or more short stories published in *Time and Tide* during the early years. A testament to the rise of a new generation of professional modern women writers in the post-war years, many of these writers would also shape the next phase of *Time and Tide*'s development from 1928.

From Fleet Street to Bloomsbury: *Time and Tide*'s 'Literary Turn' (1928–1935)

During the years 1928 to 1935 *Time and Tide* drew more widely on networks associated with the generation of modern women novelists who began appearing in its pages during the 1920s than upon the suffrage networks of an older generation that had formed a major contributor-base during the early years. In 1926 Winifred Holtby (aged 28) had become the youngest member of *Time and Tide*'s Board of Directors, and she played a pivotal role in the periodical's development. In 1927 E.M. Delafield joined the Board and became *Time and Tide*'s most popular contributor of sketches and comic writing with the publication of her *Diary of a Provincial Lady* in serial form from December 1929. Two contributors from the suffrage generation who continued to write regularly for *Time and Tide* were Cicely Hamilton and Christopher St John; but the suffrage signature was much less in evidence in this period, marking a shift in emphasis following the conclusion of women's struggle for the vote.[23] For Lady Rhondda, who took over the periodical's editorship from Helen Archdale in the summer of 1926, the successful passage of the Equal Franchise Act in 1928 marked the point when feminists were released from the necessity of fighting for political equality and could begin to seize in earnest their rightful position alongside men in the world of public affairs. Deliberately seeking to widen the periodical's appeal beyond a feminist readership, Rhondda turned *Time and Tide* into a less woman-focused, more general-audience paper competitive with such weeklies as the *New Statesman*, placing it in the forefront of the leading weekly reviews of the day.[24]

An important element of *Time and Tide*'s expansion was its increasingly literary focus. In October 1928 the periodical increased in size (from twenty-four to thirty-two pages) in order to deal 'as fully as possible with all aspects of current affairs, *and especially with books and literary subjects*' [my emphasis], and raised its price (from fourpence to sixpence) in line with other leading weekly reviews.[25] Towards the end of this period *Time and Tide* expanded still further, issuing the first of its Monthly Double Numbers in October 1934, comprising sixty-four pages including a thirty-two page literary supplement. (Its second Double Number in November 1934 was in excess of one hundred pages.) In order to deal with this increased literary content *Time and Tide* appointed its first literary editor, R. Ellis Roberts, in 1933, and drew on a larger body of reviewers, male and female. Women reviewers of fiction and poetry in this period include Theodora Bosanquet (who took over the periodical's literary editorship in 1935), Vera Brittain, the modernist writer Mary Butts, Helen Fletcher (who later developed a career as a film critic), the English critic, memoirist and essayist Olive Heseltine, the popular Irish writer Nora Hoult, Naomi Mitchison, the poet E.J. Scovell, the journalist Edith Shackleton (who later joined *Time and Tide*'s staff as drama critic), Clara Smith (assistant to Theodora Bosanquet), the Welsh novelist Hilda Vaughan, and Sylvia Townsend Warner. Another contributor, Antonia White, also wrote regular theatre criticisms for a short period in 1934.

Time and Tide's 'literary turn' has been read as a dilution, even abandonment, of the periodical's early feminist identity.[26] But this assessment fails to account for *Time and Tide*'s more complex manoeuvres within the literary and periodical marketplace, manoeuvres that may be read as feminist interventions in a cultural sphere marked by modernism's London-based 'institutionalization' and 'accession to cultural legitimacy'.[27] Specifically, *Time and Tide* remained a female-run review at a time when its competitors (such as the *New Statesman*) were very male-dominated, and it continued to promote the work of women writers subordinated to the cultures of modernism. Jane Dowson has drawn attention to the significance of *Time and Tide* for women poets in the 1930s.[28] Among those whose poetry was published in *Time and Tide* between 1928 and 1935 were Valentine Ackland, Stella Benson, Theodora Bosanquet, Frances Cornford, Stella Gibbons, Winifred Holtby, Sylvia Lynd, Naomi Mitchison, Hilda Reid, Vita Sackville-West and Sylvia Townsend Warner. Later it also published poetry by, among others, the American poet May Sarton and the Somerville graduate Margaret Stanley-Wrench. The periodical was also of special significance for what Nicola Humble has termed the 'feminine middlebrow' novelist.[29] New contributors of short stories in these years include Elizabeth Bowen, Kate O' Brien, Naomi Mitchison, Jean Rhys, Helen Simpson, Doreen Wallace, Sylvia Townsend Warner and Dorothy Whipple. While recent years have seen the rise of scholarly interest in these and other writers of middlebrow fiction, the feminist reception of this work in *Time and Tide* has still to receive sustained critical attention.[30]

At the same time that *Time and Tide* provided a platform for middlebrow authors it was also deliberately staking out a more highbrow position in the periodical marketplace in a bid for cultural legitimacy and authority. This re-positioning is graphically illustrated by the relocation of *Time and Tide*'s offices, in May 1929, from Fleet Street to Bloomsbury, a move that symbolically marks a crossing of the art/commerce, literature/journalism divide. *Time and Tide*'s announcement of its move 'to a house of its own at 32 Bloomsbury Street' carries a Woolfian echo which is resonant of its new highbrow aspirations (excerpts of *A Room of One's Own* were published in *Time and Tide* later the same year).[31] The article was illustrated by the Bloomsbury artist Gwen Raverat who contributed weekly art criticisms from this date, a further indication of the periodical's orientation towards modernist hierarchies of cultural value. Woolf's signature first appeared in *Time and Tide* in 1928, the year Bonnie Kime Scott identifies as the *annus mirabilis* for female modernism.[32] In the same year, *Time and Tide* carried articles by another representative of the female avant-garde, Edith Sitwell, and Rebecca West returned more prominently to *Time and Tide*'s pages, contributing the first of several essays of literary criticism.[33] Harnessing Bloomsbury and female modernism in this way, *Time and Tide* apparently sought to increase its reputation in literary London. Certainly, and in contrast with the early years, in and after 1928 *Time and Tide* sought to include modernist writers in its periodical community. Writing to Holtby in October 1933 Lady Rhondda commented that some of the content in a recent issue of *Time and Tide* was '[not] good enough for a literary number which all the highbrows read and criticise'.[34] By the end of this period *Time and Tide* was also carrying the male modernist signatures of Wyndham Lewis, T.S. Eliot, and Ezra Pound.

At the same time as this increased orientation towards modernist cultures, *Time and Tide* adopted George Bernard Shaw (representative of the Edwardian generation modernism defined itself against) as a kind of figurehead for the periodical.[35] Lady Rhondda later recalled how early in 1929 she and Winifred Holtby decided 'to change the slant of the paper a bit, to give it a rather broader base' and planned for 22 February 1929 a bumper number featuring George Bernard Shaw as a star contributor. From this issue the paper carried for a time a new tag in its masthead, 'Politics, Literature, Art', further underscoring *Time and Tide*'s new cultural emphasis, and according to Rhondda it was 'that issue with that grand G. B. S. in it [that] put *Time and Tide* on the map'.[36] For all his identification with feminism, journalism and politics, Shaw's high cultural stature was still guaranteed to attract a highbrow readership (letters from Rhondda to Shaw comment more than once on his extraordinary influence on sales).[37] But he also preserves an important link with the past and with a literary and journalistic tradition based on a commitment to the public sphere. In a drawing entitled 'Saint Bernard Comes to Bloomsbury', which accompanied an account of Shaw's attendance at a 'house-warming luncheon' in November 1929, the famous playwright stands at the window of *Time and Tide*'s Bloomsbury offices with a copy of *The Apple Cart* under his arm.[38]

According to one of Shaw's early biographers, this play, the first Shaw had written for five years, 'reveals the political faith of George Bernard Shaw more plainly than any other piece he wrote'.[39] *Time and Tide*'s move to Bloomsbury thus transforms the very spaces of modernism it newly occupies; by adopting Shaw as its patron 'Saint', *Time and Tide* both sustained its early endorsement of male feminism, and maintained a political writing tradition at the heart of its 'literary turn'.

Such material and textual manoeuvres point to a complex negotiation of literary culture that by no means marks a capitulation to modernist hierarchies of cultural value. An article published by *Time and Tide* in December 1928, contributed pseudonymously by Winifred Holtby, represents another important intervention in relation to modernism's domination of the literary field. The article is called 'Parnassus in Academe. Novelists at Oxford'. Identifying Oxford University as a home of poetry, literature and learning that had 'scattered since the war a shower of literary talent over England', it presents a group profile of Hilda Reid, Margaret Kennedy, Naomi Mitchison, Vera Brittain, Sylvia Thompson, and Winifred Holtby herself.[40] All, with the exception of Mitchison, who began but did not complete a degree in Science at Oxford, were former students of Somerville, and, with the exception of Kennedy, all were contributors to *Time and Tide* in these years. In this celebration of women writers whose work was accorded little value by modernist critics, Holtby's article implicitly positions Oxford as a female rival to its male competitor, Cambridge, seat of the Cambridge School of literary criticism which was to play a major role in the institutionalisation of modernism in the coming decade.[41] Significantly, Cambridge University still refused to grant degrees to women, an issue on which *Time and Tide* had been calling upon the government to intervene from the early 1920s, in contrast with Oxford University which had made the progressive decision to award degrees to women in 1921.[42] In another article published in *Time and Tide* in July 1929, Holtby, writing under the same pseudonym, paid tribute to the achievements of Somerville's graduates in the fifty years since the college was founded.[43] Mapping another tradition of women's education, professionalism and writing, these articles carve out a space for a generation of women writers that even female modernism would play a part in obscuring.

'I Cannot Keep my Thoughts from the World Situation': *Time and Tide*'s 'Sociological Turn' (1935–1939)

Tragically, in September 1935 Winifred Holtby died, aged 37, leaving a significant hole in *Time and Tide*'s periodical community. Letters from *Time and*

Tide writers and readers poured in over several weeks, testifying to Holtby's influence on the lives and minds of those who knew her, while a memorial essay by Lady Rhondda revealed just how central she had been to the periodical's development since she joined its Board of Directors in 1926.[44] On 12 October 1935, *Time and Tide* announced 'A New Departure': 'The progressive review in 1935 has [...] to be radical in its book-out-look' the editorial declared. '*Time and Tide* is therefore going, for the time being, to have a sociological outlook and this particularly, in its book section.'[45] *Time and Tide*'s 'sociological turn' represents a significant shift from the paper's interests and interventions in the literary sphere from 1928, and registers a quickening sense – at the height of the Abyssinia crisis – of the gravity of a world situation heading once again towards war. In May 1938 Lady Rhondda would write in one of the periodical's regular columns that 'I cannot keep my thoughts from the world situation', and leading articles throughout this period continued to turn *Time and Tide* into a less woman-focused, more internationally-orientated journal for a liberal-left intellectual public.[46] While the journal continued to draw upon feminist and literary networks established in earlier years, many of its writers turned increasingly from feminist and literary subjects to more broadly social, political and economic concerns. For example, in August and September 1935 Rebecca West, recently returned from the United States, contributed a series of articles on President Roosevelt's 'New Deal'; in December 1936, two months into Stalin's first Great Purge, *Time and Tide* published sketches from a forthcoming book by E.M. Delafield commissioned by an American publisher to write on the 'lighter side of Russian life'.[47]

Alongside its interventions in the cultural sphere prior to October 1935, *Time and Tide* had been establishing its political reputation, and Winifred Holtby was instrumental in this. After Holtby's death the Labour MP Ellen Wilkinson, who had contributed articles and book reviews since December 1930, assumed a larger role in the periodical's coverage of political affairs, and of the rise of fascism and unemployment especially. Other women writers who contributed to *Time and Tide*'s political pages in these years include the Yorkshire novelist Lettice Cooper, who joined the staff in 1938 and introduced a number of features on provincial England, Phoebe Fenwick Gaye, assistant editor from 1932 to 1936, Cicely Hamilton and the journalist and writer Odette Keun. Numerous women writers also appear in *Time and Tide*'s correspondence columns in response to the unfolding political crises of this decade. They include Valentine Ackland, Phyllis Bottome, Storm Jameson, Rose Macaulay, Naomi Mitchison, Helena M. Swanwick, Sylvia Townsend Warner and Rebecca West. Women writers' engagement with the wider political landscape of the 1930s belongs to the long-recognised politicisation of writing in this decade, but little attention has been awarded to *Time and Tide*'s involvement in this sphere.[48] As Maria DiCenzo and Leila Ryan observe, women's periodicals are rarely considered as part of the spectrum of sources when it comes to political history: 'There is a tendency to ghettoize feminist media [...] limiting the scope and impact of these discursive arenas and obscuring their contribution to wider political discourses.'[49] An analysis of *Time and Tide*'s interventions in the big political issues of the day is beyond the scope of this article, and deserves further attention.[50]

As a women's periodical, *Time and Tide* has also been overlooked in accounts of the British left in literature. For example, even Andy Croft's important study of the British literary left does not include *Time and Tide* in the index, although male-edited periodicals such as the *Left Review* and the *New Statesman* are frequently cited. In fact, during the 1930s several of the writers discussed by Croft were regular contributors of book reviews to *Time and Tide*, among them Ralph Bates, Geoffrey Gorer, Graham Greene, James Hanley, Malcolm Muggeridge, George Orwell and Raymond Postgate. One left-wing writer Croft does not mention is John Brophy, a Yorkshire ex-serviceman, socialist, and prolific journalist and novelist, who contributed regular reviews of 'New Novels' in *Time and Tide* between 1935 and 1939. Brophy frequently used his column to argue for the importance of the novel as an art form and for its social and political value. For example, in one review he defended 'the dignity and importance of the novel' and protested against the low ranking accorded to novels by editors of 'serious' periodicals who 'cram[ming] the notices of four or more novels into the space devoted to a single memoir and thrust[ing] the poor fiction reviewer among the end pages'.[51] While he claimed to have no 'special grouse against *Time and Tide*, which simply conforms to a custom at least two centuries old', he criticised nevertheless the assumption, implicit in the new 'sociological outlook' adopted by *Time and Tide* in its book section, 'that a novel cannot be a "serious" book'. Brophy's reviews clearly belong to what Croft has described as 'the intervention in the life of the novel by the British Left', but residing in *Time and Tide* they have been left out of both political and literary history.[52]

Time and Tide was also important for its publication of creative work by women writers on the left. New contributors of short stories in these years include the American novelist Kay Boyle, and two younger voices in English literature: Pamela Hansford Johnson, whose first of twenty-seven novels was published in 1935, and the Jewish Somerville graduate Marghanita Laski, whose first novel would be published in 1944. A more obscure contributor was Winifred Williams, a writer from the north of England whom *Time and Tide* 'discover[ed]' in June 1935.[53] In several stories *Time and Tide* published in this period Williams represented the lives of working men and women in hard-hitting detail: a young female worker in a beauty salon who becomes pregnant during an affair with a married man and undergoes an illegal abortion; an impoverished man employed at five shillings a day for the humiliating job of carrying a grotesque *papier-mâché* 'Head' of a Conservative Party candidate; a poverty-stricken ex-soldier who commits suicide by gassing himself in the cellar.[54] This fiction is important to recuperative work on working-class writing that has brought greater prominence to men than to women writers. Evidence of the vitality of working-class women's writing in a periodical more commonly associated with the middle-class middlebrow, Williams's stories also demonstrate that male-edited publications such as *Left Review* were not the only periodicals that introduced working-class writing to a wide readership.

Sounding a different note, the contributions of *Time and Tide*'s literary editor, Theodora Bosanquet, remind us that not all writers subscribed to the politicisation of art and literature in this decade. Formerly the secretary of Henry James, Bosanquet was a highbrow literary intellectual, author of books on James, the French symbolist poet Paul Valéry and the nineteenth-century English feminist Harriet Martineau. She was also the secretary of the International Federation of University Women, through which she and Lady Rhondda first became acquainted in 1922.[55] Bosanquet's contributions to *Time and Tide* – book reviews and extended essays in the periodical's 'Men and Books' section – include discussions of T.S. Eliot, Virginia Woolf, and W.B. Yeats, and throughout this writing she maintained a high modernist separation of art and politics that contrasts with *Time and Tide*'s reviewers from the literary left. In a review of Woolf's novel *The Years*, for example, she defended Woolf's 'persistent preoccupation with the luminous glory of life' and (anticipating indignant protest from 'the class-conscious and guilt-ridden propagandists of the present age') concluded that:

> In *The Years* [...] we are in contact not only with a first-rate novelist [...] but also with a great lyrical poet. It is not a poet's function (*pace* Mr. Auden and co.) to offer us a sociological tract but to give us more abundant life.[56]

Bosanquet's resistance to the cultural dominance of the Auden generation underlines once again the multiple discourses that *Time and Tide* as a periodical text kept going. *Time and Tide* reviewed the work of 'Mr Auden and co.' and occasionally carried their signatures.[57] But Bosanquet's reviews also direct us to another, female, generation with a different set of interests that coalesced around the traditions of spiritualism and mysticism. For Bosanquet, a long-time member of the Society for Psychical Research, and editor of its journal during the Second World War, these interests were manifest in her practice of automatic writing throughout the 1930s that had connections with surrealism, and with the revival of mediumship during the interwar years.[58] According to Bette London, mediumship held an important place in women's culture in this period, and attracted in particular women from middle-class backgrounds with 'intellectual, artistic, and professional aspirations'. As 'occupations' and 'points of entrée into exclusive intellectual and artistic circles' modern practices of mediumship were, says London, 'important avenues for women's professionalization and mental development'.[59] For Bosanquet, mediumship appears to have facilitated or at least meshed in interesting ways with her professional work as literary editor for *Time and Tide*, providing yet more ways to consider the construction of women's professional writing identities in this periodical.

More cultural recovery work is required to map the female networks and practices associated with mediumship, automatism and also religious and mystical writing between the wars. Two more writers introduced to *Time and Tide* by Bosanquet were Renée Haynes, author of a history of the Society for Psychical Research, published in 1982, and the religious writer Evelyn Underhill, both book reviewers from 1936 and 1937 respectively, who shared Bosanquet's interests in psychical research, spiritualism and mysticism. Together this group represents a different response to a world in crisis than that of *Time and Tide*'s writers on the literary left. Haynes, in a poem dedicated 'To Evelyn Underhill' published in *Time and Tide* in December 1934, used Christ's nativity to illuminate capitalism's crushing stranglehold on a society that had lost religious and moral direction.[60] Underhill, a prolific writer on religion and mysticism, whose 1911 book *Mysticism* influenced T.S. Eliot, wrote reviews of religious books which reflect her pacifism, a discourse that found expression in other parts of the paper even though by the time war broke out the periodical had editorially distanced itself from this position.[61] Bosanquet wrote a lengthy review of Virginia Woolf's *Three Guineas*, widely recognised as the 'ur-text' of feminist anti-war writing.[62] But as Phyllis Lassner observes, 'Woolf's was not a lone voice but one of many in a vital feminist debate on war and fascism in the thirties'.[63] While literary scholarship has gone some way to recovering the voices of writers such as Sylvia Townsend Warner, no longer a contributor to *Time and Tide* at this time, it remains virtually silent on such writers as Bosanquet, Haynes and Underhill.

The war years saw a re-grouping of *Time and Tide*'s writers. From November 1939 to January 1940 a protracted correspondence between Naomi Mitchison and Rebecca West on the subject of 'War Aims' highlighted widening divisions on the left. Mitchison severed her connections with *Time and Tide* (and London); West remained, along with other regular writers of earlier years including E.M. Delafield and Cicely Hamilton. Some old contributors returned to *Time and Tide*'s pages during the war, including Sylvia Lynd, Rose Macaulay and Naomi Royde-Smith. New writers for *Time and Tide* during the war years include

Margery Allingham, a contributor of book reviews from 1938, Dorothy Sayers and Stevie Smith. A particularly significant writer for *Time and Tide* who first appeared in the paper's pages in the 1940s was the historian Cicely Veronica Wedgwood, who played an increasingly central role in the periodical, replacing Bosanquet as literary editor in 1943. The paper's fortunes, however, gradually declined, and *Time and Tide* did not long survive Lady Rhondda's death in 1958.

The first two decades of *Time and Tide*'s existence remain the most fascinating for the window they open up onto cultural debates of the period. Demonstrating an engagement with modernism by women writers since dissociated from its movements, this periodical also shows that modernism does not have the kind of unchallenged cultural authority that has often been claimed for it. Specifically, I have shown that *Time and Tide* reveals the myriad ways in which its female contributors pursued and advocated different political and aesthetic agendas, and the ways in which they resisted their marginalisation as modernism secured its cultural dominance. A testament in particular to the rise of the professional woman writer between the two world wars, *Time and Tide* offers fertile ground for tracing 'the importance of everything else' left out of modernist accounts.

Acknowledgements

The British Academy has provided generous support for my research on *Time and Tide*. I would like to thank the members of the History of Feminism Network who commented on an early draft of this article. I am particularly grateful to Faith Binckes, Lucy Delap, and Maria DiCenzo who provided generous comments on later drafts. I would also like to thank Ben Harker for inviting me to contribute to this issue and for his useful editorial suggestions.

Notes

1   E.J. Scovell, 'The Modern Ghost Hunt', 18 November 1933, p. 1388.
2   Ann Ardis, *New Women, New Novels: Feminism and Early Modernism* (New Brunswick: Rutgers University Press, 1990) and Gaye Tuchman, *Edging Women Out: Victorian Novelists, Publishers and Social Change* (London: Routledge, 1989).
3   Here I follow Lucy Delap who uses the term 'periodical community' to refer to 'the material, cultural, and intellectual milieu of a periodical or group of related periodicals'. '*The Freewoman*, Periodical Communities, and the Feminist Reading Public', *Princeton University Library Chronicle*, 61.2 (Winter 2000), p. 234.
4   Occasional contributions were drawn from leading figures of both the militant and constitutional wings of the suffrage movement, including Mrs Pethick-Lawrence of the WSPU and Millicent Fawcett of the NUWSS.

5. Sowon S. Park, 'Doing Justice to the Real Girl: The Women Writers' Suffrage League', in Claire Eustance, Joan Ryan and Laura Ugolini, eds, *A Suffrage Reader: Charting Directions in British Suffrage History* (Leicester: Leicester University Press, 2000), p. 92.
6. Editorial note introducing this feature in the first issue, 14 May 1920, p. 7.
7. Anonymous author of a 'Personalities and Powers' feature on the Scottish educationist and suffragist Louisa Innes Lumsden. 5 November 1920, p. 523.
8. Hamilton was MP for Blackburn from 1929–1931. Her biographical subjects include influential figures in the Labour movement: Ramsay MacDonald (1923), Margaret Bondfield (1924), Mary Macarthur (1925), and Arthur Henderson (1938).
9. Jane Dowson and Alice Entwistle, *A History of Twentieth-Century British Women's Poetry* (Cambridge: Cambridge University Press, 2005), p. 18.
10. Jason Harding, *The Criterion: Cultural Politics and Periodical Networks in Inter-War Britain* (Oxford: Oxford University Press, 2002), p. 1.
11. 'Political Fiction', 12 November 1920, pp. 550–51 (p. 550).
12. 'The Economic Man', 14 August 1925, p. 792.
13. See Patrick Collier's discussion of the literature/journalism divide in *Modernism on Fleet Street* (Aldershot: Ashgate, 2006), pp. 26–7.
14. Patrick Collier observes that newspapers frequently function as a 'rhetorical enemy' in modernist writings of the period. Collier, p. 4. Rose Macaulay's relationship to journalism was more ambivalent than the other writers mentioned here. See Collier, pp. 137–67.
15. 'Journalism Meets Modernism', in Bonnie Kime Scott, ed., *Gender and Modernism: New Geographies, Complex Intersections* (Urbana and Chicago: University of Illinois Press, 2007), p. 188.
16. 'Teacups and Turbines: Negotiating Modernity in the Interwar Women's Professional Magazine'. Paper given at the 10th annual conference of the Modern Studies Association, Nashville, Tennessee, November 2008. I am indebted to Alice Staveley for her insights into the role played by *Time and Tide*, alongside a host of women's professional magazines, in constructing the professional woman as a specifically modern phenomenon.
17. 'Transatlantic Print Culture: The Anglo-American Feminist Press and Emerging "Modernities"', in Ann Ardis and Patrick Collier, *Transatlantic Print Culture, 1880–1940: Emerging Media, Emerging Modernisms* (Basingstoke: Palgrave Macmillan, 2008), p. 49.
18. Staveley has located these advertisements in such magazines as *The Woman Engineer*.
19. By the 1920s the image of woman as worker was not confined to feminist print culture, as Fiona Hackney's study of the mainstream press and women's magazines has shown. 'Women are News: British Women's Magazines 1919–1939', in Ardis and Collier, pp. 114–33.
20. 'The Minute Hand', 8 October 1920, p. 454.
21. Maria DiCenzo, 'Feminism, Theatre Criticism, and the Modern Drama', *South Carolina Review* 25.1 (Spring 2008), p. 44.
22. Delap and DiCenzo, p. 52.
23. This shift is also reflected in the disappearance from 1928 of generic features shared with suffrage journalism, including 'Personalities and Powers' and 'In the Tideway'.
24. See Lady Rhondda's autobiography, *This Was My World* (London: Macmillan, 1933), p. 299. This shift in focus should not be seen as an abandonment of its feminist position. As Michelle Tusan has convincingly argued, by appropriating the weekly review format Lady Rhondda succeeded in placing women in the vanguard of mainstream political culture. *Women Making News: Gender and Journalism in Modern Britain* (Urbana and Chicago: University of Illinois Press, 2005), pp. 229–33.
25. 'Review of the Week', 5 October 1928, p. 905. The new format took effect from the next issue on 12 October 1928.

26 Dale Spender states that *Time and Tide* 'drifted more towards an arts and literary review' which is for her 'a matter of some regret'. Dale Spender, *Time and Tide Wait for No Man* (London: Pandora, 1984), p. 24.
27 Michael Levenson identifies T.S. Eliot's founding of the *Criterion* in 1922 as modernism's coming of age 'because it exemplifies the institutionalization of the movement, the accession to cultural legitimacy'. Cited by Harding, p. 1. Harding posits that 1926, the year Eliot launched the *New Criterion*, is 'a better marker of modernism's London "institutionalization" and "cultural legitimacy"', p. 15.
28 Jane Dowson, *Women's Poetry of the 1930s: A Critical Anthology* (London: Routledge, 1996).
29 Nicola Humble, *The Feminine Middlebrow Novel, 1920s to 1950s: Class, Domesticity, and Bohemianism* (Oxford: Oxford University Press, 2001).
30 The difficulty of defining the 'middlebrow' becomes apparent here. Bowen and Rhys, for example, are among a number of women writers of the period who have been incorporated since within a feminist modernist canon.
31 Anon., 'Moving House', 10 May 1929, p. 547.
32 Bonnie Kime Scott, *Refiguring Modernism: The Women of 1928* (Bloomington and Indianapolis: Indiana University Press, 1995).
33 Rebecca West is one of Scott's three central figures in her study of female modernism. West's extended literary critical essay *The Strange Necessity*, which included a discussion of James Joyce, was published in 1928.
34 Unpublished letter, 17 October 1933, Winifred Holtby Collection, Hull Local Studies Library.
35 Shaw was also a figurehead for an earlier generation of literary/political periodicals, the *New Age* in particular.
36 Lady Rhondda, 'Reminiscences of an Editor', 17 May 1941, p. 398.
37 George Bernard Shaw Collection, Harry Ransom Humanities Research Center, University of Texas at Austin.
38 'Saint Bernard on All Saints Day. Bernard Shaw Drinks Our Health', 8 November 1929, p. 1334.
39 John Ervine, *Bernard Shaw* (London: Constable and Co., 1956), p. 516.
40 28 December 1928, p. 1272. Holtby writes as 'GREC'.
41 Cambridge English professor F.R. Leavis extended his influence though the journal *Scrutiny* which he founded with his wife, Q.D. Leavis, in 1932. His *Mass Civilization and Minority Culture* (1930) and *New Bearings in English Poetry* (1932) also aligned him with the high modernist tradition.
42 On 29 June 1923 *Time and Tide* published a leading article in which it criticised the government for giving state aid to a university which continued to exclude half the population.
43 GREC, 'The Somerville Tradition: After Fifty Years', 5 July 1929, pp. 810–12.
44 'Winifred Holtby', 5 October 1935, pp. 1391–3.
45 'A New Departure', 12 October 1935, p. 1422.
46 'Notes on the Way', 14 May 1938, p. 663.
47 'Special Investigation', 26 December 1936, p. 1838.
48 An exception is Johanna Alberti's 'British Feminists and Anti-Fascism in the 1930s', in Sybil Oldfield, ed., *This Working-Day World: Women's Lives and Culture(s) in Britain 1914–1945* (London: Taylor and Francis, 1994), pp. 111–22.
49 'Neglected News: Women and Print Media, 1890–1928', in Charles R. Acland, ed., *Residual Media* (Minneapolis: University of Minnesota Press, 2007), p. 248.
50 A key event, of course, was Spain. *Time and Tide* maintained a non-interventionist position in contrast with more radical left-wing periodicals including the *Left Review* and *New Verse*

which declared their support for the Republicans in Spain. See Alvin Sullivan, *British Literary Magazines: The Modern Age 1914–84* (Westport: Greenwood Press, 1986), p. 538.
51 'New Novels', 3 April 1937, pp. 436–7.
52 Andy Croft, *Red Letter Days: British Fiction in the 1930s* (London: Lawrence and Wishart, 1990), p. 25.
53 *Time and Tide* drew attention to its 'discovery' of Winifred Williams in 'Notes on Some Contributors', 12 October 1935, p. 1436.
54 'No Nerve', 21 March 1936; 'The Head', 8 August 1936; 'Gas', 31 October 1936.
55 Shirley Eoff, *Viscountess Rhondda: Equalitarian Feminist* (Columbus: Ohio State University Press, 1991), p. 113.
56 'Mrs Woolf's New Novel', 13 March 1937, p. 353.
57 *Time and Tide* published a poem by Auden, 'Europe 1936', on 23 May 1936. *Time and Tide* also published articles by Stephen Spender in October 1934 and December 1936.
58 On Bosanquet and automatic writing see Pamela Thurschwell, *Literature, Technology and Magical Thinking, 1880–1920* (Cambridge: Cambridge University Press, 2001). On the relationship between mediumship and modernist cultures see Bette London, 'Mediumship, Automatism, and Modernist Authorship', in Bonnie Kime Scott, ed., *Gender in Modernism: New Geographies, Complex Intersections* (Urbana and Chicago: University of Illinois Press, 2007), pp. 622–32.
59 London, pp. 625–6.
60 'Nativity', 8 December 1934, pp. 1568–9.
61 In June 1939 James Hanley's defence of conscientious objectors in *Time and Tide*'s 'Notes on the Way' column was prefaced by an editorial note disagreeing emphatically with his views. 17 June 1939.
62 'Men and Books', 4 June 1938, pp. 778–90.
63 Phyllis Lassner, *British Women Writers of World War Two* (Basingstoke: Macmillan, 1997), p. 29.

'Ours will be a dynamic contribution': The Struggle by Diasporic Artists for a Voice in British Theatre in the 1930s and 1940s
Colin Chambers

Recovering cultural production that has been confined to the margins of conventional history can not only validate valuable discoveries but can also reconstitute the very history that has previously ignored them by revealing the complex interplay between the periphery and the centre. In the process, the notion of being on the edge can recover its metaphorical association of vibrant innovation, and the accepted mainstream/fringe model of shaping the past can be challenged by counter-posing an alternative history. The struggle of the non-white subject peoples of Britain's empire to find their own voice in the British theatre offers such an alternative. It is a struggle for individual and collective self-expression, intertwined with, and reflecting, a wider struggle against racism and for national independence, and it is a struggle that has provided British theatre with dynamic forms and themes often lost to, or suppressed in, standard theatre historiography.[1]

This struggle within British theatre inevitably intersected at certain moments with radical politics. It gained momentum in the 1930s and the 1940s (against the backdrop of anti-colonial struggle, fascism, the invasion of Ethiopia, and Spain's civil war), before being boosted as a consequence of post-war immigration. The struggle then flourished in the last quarter of the twentieth century when extreme right-wing attacks on 'ethnic communities' and aggressively racist policing drew a concerted riposte from besieged communities. Only at this juncture was it possible to talk of the existence – however fraught and fragile – of an autonomous British diasporic theatre, though how it should be defined was, and remains, disputed both by the practitioners themselves and by commentators. (For the purposes of this essay, the term diasporic refers to the non-white diaspora.) Here is not the place to negotiate the terminological minefield created by empire, but the unease and impermanence of linguistic practice in this area needs to be noted. Rejecting the notion of ethnic arts deployed by state funding agencies in the 1970s, the practitioners preferred the term Black theatre. It carried a capital 'B' to indicate a political notion that embraced common strands of experience and resistance among the former colonised peoples and their British-born successors. This usage was contested by those of South Asian origin and did not survive long. It was replaced by black (lower case 'b') and Asian to reflect the dominant heritage strands, African, Caribbean and Asian, or simply black as the convenient short-hand catch-all.[2] With the state adopting a diversity agenda in the 1990s came increasing specificity – South Asian and East Asian, for example – accompanied by use of the generic descriptor diasporic (which lacks the specificity of the heritage strands and their relationship to colour, and is problematic for successive generations of the British born). There was also continuing reluctance by many of the artists to be defined by any sociopolitical label.

The existence of this diasporic theatre (however complex the changing and challenged vocabulary) stimulated scholarship within and beyond the academy to begin a process revealing and exploring the black (broadly defined as non-white) presence in radio, film, television and theatre. Within that wider discourse was closer examination of particular performance arenas, whether, for example, black Edwardian entertainers, contemporary female black writing, or British South-Asian theatre.[3] Continuing into the twenty-first century, this process of recovery and investigation has overlapped with developments in deconstruction and cultural theory (e.g. Derrida, Foucault, Bourdieu, Hall, Bhabha) and its examination and theorising of outsider or marginal practice. As a small contribution to the process of recuperation, this documenting essay forms part of a larger personal project to construct a continuous (though not teleological) British theatrical history that reaches to the present from the representations of the Other in the medieval period.[4]

The focus of this essay is the activity of diasporic artists in London in the seedbed period of the 1930s to the 1940s before post-war immigration from the Caribbean, South Asia and East Africa changed the demographic and created the critical mass necessary for the establishment of an autonomous diasporic theatre. Prior to World War One, while there is evidence of the diasporic presence in a variety of entertainments in Britain, there is little in the theatre outside of musical performance, with notable exceptions such as the nineteenth-century African-American actor Ira Aldridge. The only collective activity of any note comes at the beginning of the twentieth century within the Indian student community and in the activities of the amateur Indian Art and Dramatic Society (IADS). The IADS sought to foster understanding between 'east and west' by asserting India's culture to be as rich as Europe's through multi-cultural productions of plays from the ancient Sanskrit repertoire and contemporary work by the celebrated Bengali writer Rabindranath Tagore.[5] The IADS faded away in the 1920s, as did the Indian Players, founded in 1922 by IADS member Niranjan Pal to present his play *The Goddess*. The play tells the story of a Brahmin priest in the nineteenth century who rejects his faith for rationalism yet pronounces a beggar woman with whom he is in love to be the incarnation of the goddess Kali. Despite being unhappy with the deception, she agrees to appear as Kali in order to please him and she then commits suicide to atone for her sacrilege. The Indian Players performed *The Goddess* for two matinee appearances in the West End at the Duke of York's Theatre with an all-Indian cast speaking in English. Clearly *The Goddess* chimed with rather than challenged English notions of an intriguing if backward and mystical India because the production subsequently also played at the Ambassadors and Aldwych theatres for more than sixty performances. Even *The Times* noted that, although the play was described as modern, 'From this it must not be understood that it has direct concern with the political problems of today'.[6] Pal also wrote *The Magic Crystal*, a conventional and anodyne farce in an English setting which uses a visionary Indian as a key plot device. It toured England in 1924 before Pal returned to India in 1929 where he became a distinguished film writer.

It was not until the 1930s that the British diasporic voice began to be heard again, when – without wishing to suggest a unified or homogenised grouping – the slow and uneven formation of a community of shared interests can be seen. Unsurprisingly, this occurred not in the dominant commercial theatre but in amateur and/or semi-professional drama. This distinct voice was supported by an embryonic network of social, cultural and welfare groups, such as the Negro Welfare Association and the League of Coloured Peoples (LCP), a clutch of student hostels playing host to arrivals from India, Africa, the Caribbean and further afield, and informal cultural centres such as the Florence Mills Social Club. The LCP, founded in 1931 as an integrationist, gradualist Pan-African body, open to all races but overwhelmingly with a black membership and under black leadership, had twelve centres in Britain at its height. It also published a journal, *The Keys*, which supported campaigns, reported social activities, including dances, concerts, garden parties, and cricket matches, and addressed issues of representation of black people in cultural forms (it carried poems, book reviews and occasional theatre and film items). In November 1933, the LCP took the brave and unusual step of producing a play. Even more uncommon, the play was written by a woman.

At What a Price, a formally conventional comedy written by Jamaican Una Marson when she was twenty-six, deals with women's experience in a male culture; spirited but naive young Ruth, daughter to a weak mother and patriarchal father, leaves her middle-class, countryside home to work as a stenographer in Kingston, falls for the charms of her white boss and has to return to her parents, pregnant, deceived, rueful. Though her attempt at independence fails, the play applauds her feistiness and rejection of women's domestic marital subjugation. Mounting *At What a Price* was a huge undertaking, which Marson led. It is a four-act play, which calls for some twenty actors playing Jamaicans. Marson took the main role and was directed by Clifford Norman, who had to draw on people with little or no acting experience from different cultural backgrounds –

their original home was listed next to their name in the programme: Bermuda, British Guiana, England, Gold Coast, India, Italy, Jamaica, St Lucia, and West Africa, an indication of the spread of the diaspora and LCP membership. Of the cast, several went on to distinguished careers, including the future British Communist and noted Ghanaian anti-colonial fighter Desmond Buckle; Eric Campbell, who became a member of the Jamaican House of Representatives for the People's National Party; Fred Degazon, Dominica's first president after independence; Keith Gordon, a barrister who became a senior judge in the Caribbean and was knighted; LCP founder Dr Harold Moody; and founding LCP executive member and LCP librarian, barrister Stella Thomas, a Nigerian of Sierra Leonean descent, Pan-African activist, the first African woman to qualify as a barrister and the first woman to be appointed a magistrate in Nigeria (in 1943).

The production began at the central London YWCA and was sufficiently successful to transfer for a three-night run in January 1934 to the 1,130-seat Scala Theatre nearby. *At What a Price* was favourably reviewed in the *Manchester Guardian*, *West African*, *Daily Herald* and elsewhere, and, though the production failed in its original aim – to raise money for the LCP – it did succeed in another aspiration, as a political statement that demonstrated cultural autonomy. As *The Keys* said, the 'all-coloured' production aimed to:

> bring home to the British public the fact that we can manage our own affairs effectively and therefore need not to be for ever under tutelage. It will also bring our own people together and help us have more confidence in ourselves, dissipate from among us any inferiority complex in ourselves, and assist us to find a basis for fuller co-operation among ourselves. Its effect must also spread overseas and be a source of inspiration to our race.[7]

Marson, described by her biographer as the first major female poet of the Caribbean and the first black feminist in Britain to speak out against racism and sexism, had come to England in 1932 and became secretary of the LCP and editor of *The Keys*.[8] Her trip was financed by the small profit she had made from the first production of *At What a Price* earlier that year at Kingston's Ward Theatre, where she was credited as co-deviser with a friend, Horace Vaz (her biographer says it was mostly her work).[9] She later wrote two more plays, neither of which were seen in Britain: another comedy, *London Calling* (published in 1937 after she had returned to Jamaica), which tells of an African prince from an imaginary colony who, as a student in Britain, has farcical encounters with the English upper classes but in the process nevertheless manages to counter the myth of black inferiority; and what is regarded as her most impressive and original play, *Pocomania* (1938), inspired by marginalised black culture, in language, folk song and dance. Her drama, however, has been overshadowed by her poetry. Although *At What a Price* represents a minor element in her output, in its assertion of female independence and black pride it echoes the central themes of better-known work, such as *Tropic Reveries* (1930), her first collection of poems, which are also set in Jamaica and explore a women's desire for self-expression and freedom. *At What a Price* also looks forward to later poetry collections, such as *Moth and the Star* (1937), which validates black definitions of value and aspiration, and *Towards the Stars* (1945), which celebrates the autonomous female. Marson became known not only as a poet but also as an activist who set up the Jamaican Save the Children Fund, worked in the Women's International League for Peace and British Commonwealth League, served as secretary to Haile Selassie, and became an important figure in British black culture: she was freelance at the BBC before gaining a full time job as programme assistant coordinating broadcasts under the title *Calling the West Indies*, later renamed *Caribbean Voices*, which was aimed at British-based Caribbean service personnel to help maintain contact with home. Marson, the first black female programme maker at the BBC, gave *Caribbean Voices* a cultural agenda, especially in her use of short stories, and it remained an important influence until it closed in the late 1950s. She returned to the Caribbean at the end of the war and continued her involvement in the anti-colonial struggle, a herald of the significant role to be played by Caribbean women such as Pearl Connor and Yvonne Brewster in the post-war development of diasporic British theatre.

In contrast to *At What a Price*, which was produced by a diasporic organisation, the other distinctive manifestations of diasporic theatrical activity in the 1930s were associated with white-led companies, most of which were on the left. A group called Left Theatre, for example, which was founded in 1934 by progressive theatre professionals, staged that year an American play *They Shall Not Die* by John Wexley (a white writer) only three months after it had finished its run in New York. The play tells the story of a notorious case in which nine young black teenagers – some as young as thirteen – were falsely convicted of raping two white women, sentenced to death and held in prison while their fate was debated through the courts. The Scottsboro Boys case, as it was known, became a rallying point for the international left in demonstrations, petitions and pamphlets as well as in plays. In Britain, colonial students, especially in the West African Students Union, were very active in the Scottsboro Defence Committee, which was chaired by Paul Robeson and Jomo Kenyatta. *They Shall Not Die*, a three-act play that moved between the court room, the death cell and the defence lawyer's office, fictionalised the case but left no doubt as to its subject: the action follows the case closely and quotations from transcripts were used in the trial scenes. An avowedly partisan play, which ends with the jury trying to make up its mind, *They Shall Not Die* attacks the repressive and racist state apparatus of the American South, criticises the response to the case of moderate black opinion and supports the Communist-led attempts to free the accused.

Left Theatre presented *They Shall Not Die* on a Sunday evening at the Holborn Empire, a huge variety venue with a capacity of almost 2,000. While London theatre managements were reported as refusing to host a benefit concert for the Scottsboro aid fund, Left Theatre invited a spokeswoman of the Defence Committee to address the audience during the interval to raise money and garner support.[10] With the Committee's cooperation, the play was performed again the following two Sundays, first at Greenwich Borough Hall and then East Ham Town Hall, at the end of which performance a resolution was moved by the local mayor and carried unanimously protesting at the trial and demanding the release of the 'boys' with compensation for their imprisonment. The production was directed by a professional Left Theatre member, André van Gyseghem, a key figure in left-wing theatre of the time who later joined the Communist Party. The black actors in the large cast included Ernest McKenzie, a socialist who attended the 1945 Pan-African Congress and established the Caribbean Bureau after the war, and, as the main defendant, Orlando Martins, who became the leading Nigerian actor in Britain. Martins's life was symptomatic: he had settled in London in 1919 and earned his living as best he could in a variety of jobs, working as a Billingsgate porter, wrestler, circus snake-charmer, night-watchman, kitchen porter, road sweeper, merchant seaman, silent film walk-on and, for Diaghilev, a ballet extra as a Nubian slave.

Another link between Left Theatre and the anti-racist struggle was the Indian-Irish actor and writer Aubrey Menon, who had set up a theatre group at University College, London with students of several nationalities 'in order to expose the character of the world they were living in'.[11] With van Gyseghem and others from Left Theatre, Menon founded the Experimental Theatre, which performed at the West End's Fortune Theatre on a Sunday evening in 1934 Menon's anti-fascist and anti-racist play *Genesis II*. It is an ambitious and sprawling reworking of the first books of the Bible that deals with the oppression of one race by another and journeys from Eden and the British Museum Reading Room to a swastika-clad German police station and an Indian tea plantation. The group subsequently found its own premises in north London where they converted a house into a 120-seat venue with a 'floating' stage, which appeared not to be fixed to the ground (it comprised two platforms at different levels and a cantilever support underneath entirely covered in black so that the audience could not see it). The project promised much. The group, which incorporated dance and music in its programme, responded to current events in Living Newspaper form as well as presenting its repertoire of plays. The initial, twenty-week, season opened with an evening that comprised three dance-drama 'News Reel' items ('Bread Queue', 'Eviction' and 'Factory'), and Menon's play *Pacific*, set on a Polynesian island and featuring Polynesian songs and dances; it was described by one critic as dealing in a semi-realistic way with 'the coloured problem' in an 'odd' production that had 'moments of interest and even power'.[12] Other offerings in the season included a classical Chinese play, *Apu Ollantay* (an Aztec drama of revolt against the Inca), classics from Tibet and Java, and Kaladisa's *Hero and Nymph* from India. The small auditorium, however, was not financially viable, and the venture soon collapsed. It is not clear how much of the programme was achieved, although one item, *The Mysterious Universe*, Menon's adaptation of the astronomer James Jeans's book, appeared at the Arts Theatre in 1935. Menon toured Britain campaigning for Indian independence with the India League before going to live and write in India.

Van Gyseghem provided another connection to the history of diasporic artists through his tenure in the 1930s as director for the Embassy Theatre, north London, where he directed Paul Robeson twice. The Embassy was one of the country's 'little' theatres, which presented a fortnightly repertoire that dealt with pressing social issues using club membership to circumvent censorship. Robeson's own political and cultural struggles epitomised the era, moving as he did from the dominant performance terrain, which he had conquered, to the alternative landscape in order to express more fully his developing political awareness. Robeson's achievements in white theatre did not make a direct contribution to British diasporic theatre, nor was he part of the British empire's diaspora, a fact that sometimes led to resentment in the job market when British-based Caribbean and African actors were overlooked in favour of him. But his figurehead role as a successful non-white actor, as catalyst and inspiration, his African heritage, and his involvement in British projects that validated diasporic values and aspirations have secured him a significant place in the history of British diasporic theatre.

Robeson had appeared to immense acclaim in the West End in the musical *Show Boat* (1928), as Othello (1930) and in Eugene O'Neill's expressionist *The Hairy Ape* (1931) before turning to the Embassy Theatre. His first appearance there came in 1933 as Jim Harris in O'Neill's *All God's Chillun Got Wings* and the second in 1935 in another white American play, *Stevedore* by Paul Peters and George Sklar. Robeson had read about this play, a hit in New York, and wanted to perform in it. *Stevedore* tells of black and white dock workers uniting to defend a black worker, Lonnie Thompson, who had complained about being cheated by his boss and was then wrongly accused of raping a white woman. The workers face a braying white mob, and Lonnie is shot dead. Another black worker takes his place to carry on the struggle: the end is only the beginning. *Stevedore* carries a clear, if optimistic and idealised, political message of unity and resistance, which appealed to Robeson. From the point of view of British diasporic theatre, although *Stevedore* was written by white Americans, its significance lies in the fact that it had a majority of black characters (three times as many as the white) who were played by black actors rather than white actors blacking up, as was still the custom, and that the black characters were seen as agents of their own lives, not just victims. Unlike O'Neill's plays, *Stevedore* connected its black characters in both class and racial terms to a broader collective experience. Lonnie's call to act is challenged by a fellow black worker: 'Lonnie says stand up and fight. How you gwine fight? What you gwine fight with? White man own dis country. White man rule it. You can't fight against him.' To which Lonnie replies: 'We can't wait for de judgement day. We can't wait till we dead and gone. We got to fight fo' de right to live. Now – now – right now.'[13] Just before Lonnie is killed, his rallying cry is:

> Dar black folks all over de country looking at us right now: dey counting on us, crying to us: 'Stand yo' ground. You fighting fo' us. You fighting fo' all of us.'[14]

The production was also important because it became a focal point for cultural expression among the diasporic population. According to a friend of Robeson's, help in casting the play came from a Miss Maukaus, an African anti-imperialist whose house was a hub for Africans in London, and from the Jamaican Pan-Africanist Amy Ashwood Garvey, the first wife of, now separated from, Marcus Garvey, who ran the Florence Mills Social Club with Trinidadian actor and musician Sam Manning. George Padmore, the Trinidadian revolutionary, introduced his friend Robert Adams, and recruited seamen and African and Caribbean students. Robeson's African-American entertainment friends also helped out: the singer John Payne was the music director, and his choir sang in the production – it seems likely he helped recruit, too, given the number of variety artists involved – and Lawrence Brown, Robeson's pianist and collaborator, acted one of the roles. The lack of a readily available pool of diasporic actors to call on was due partly to the relatively small number of the diasporic population resident in Britain and partly to the debasing roles usually on offer, which did nothing to encourage anyone who might be interested in acting. Productions like *Stevedore* helped change this situation and began to create a group of actors who, like Orlando Martins, found work as extras in film and looked to the stage for less well remunerated but more productive roles.

Following *Stevedore*, Robeson returned to an idea that had been mooted before, by the League of Coloured Peoples and others, of establishing a diasporic cultural centre. He intended to tour *Stevedore* in repertoire with *Basalik*, in which he had appeared the previous month at the small Arts Theatre, but this wooden depiction of an African chief resisting British intrusion did not last beyond its three-performance trial; the idea of a tour was dropped and with it the putative cultural centre.[15] Finding the right material, politically and artistically, was difficult for Robeson, and made more urgent when films in which he starred such as *Sanders of the River* (1935) turned out to be pro-imperialist. *They Shall Not Die* and *Stevedore* were unlike any British plays being written at the time, both in terms of political content and muscularity of language. They came from the militant American theatre of dynamic social realism, which suited Robeson, but the emerging diasporic community in Britain sought plays more closely related to its own agenda. When offered the part of the Haitian revolutionary Toussaint Louverture, leader of the first black Republic, in C.L.R. James's play of the same name, the needs of Robeson and the British diasporic community coincided.[16] James says he conceived the idea of the play in 1932, the year he left Trinidad for Britain, and finished the script by the autumn of 1934, a period during which both he and Robeson became more radical in a process that deepened during the next few years.[17] James drew on research he was doing for a book called *The Black Jacobins* and the more general *A History of Negro Revolt*, both of which were to appear in 1938.[18] He was spurred by the dual desire to counter imperial versions of history, as could be found, for example, in the programme of British events commemorating the centenary of the 1833 Emancipation Act, and to validate black achievement. James's play is both an historical re-imagining and a call to arms in the anti-colonial struggle as well as an exploration of the difficulties that this struggle throws up.

Toussaint Louverture: The Story of the Only Successful Slave Revolt in History is an ambitious, epic work in three acts running from 1791 to 1804, encapsulating the legacy of the African diaspora, which is one both of slavery and of the slaves' resistance to their oppression. Toussaint establishes a free society in the name of the French Republic, but, on behalf of the white planters, Napoleon sends a force to Haiti, and tricks Toussaint, who dies in prison. In the face of attempts to re-establish slavery, a permanent Republic is created under the leadership of another black leader, Dessalines. The play ranges in location from the forests of Haiti to the French Convention and in music from Mozart's *Don Giovanni* and African drumming to spirituals and the revolutionary songs of France. Its direct engagement with the birth of the modern European world at the time of the French Revolution challenges the history of the Enlightenment by focusing on the centrality of slavery to it. Yet the play is also conceived within an Enlightenment frame: Toussaint is a tragic hero in classical mould, though his fatal flaw is not psychological but political. He declares: 'White men see Negroes as slaves. If the Negro is to be free, he must free himself. We have courage, we have endurance, we have numbers.'[19] But he believes in the values of the Enlightenment and trusts revolutionary France, which lets him down. When Dessalines argues for total independence, Toussaint replies:

> Freedom – yes – but freedom is not everything. Dessalines, look at the state of the people. We who live here shall never see Africa again – some of us born here have never seen it. Language we have none – French is now our language. We have no education – the little that some of us know we have learnt from France. Those few of us who are Christians follow the French religion. We must stay with France as long as she does not seek to restore slavery.[20]

As Christian Hogsbjerg points out in an introduction to the play, it is only after the betrayal of Toussaint, in his last lines – 'Oh, Dessalines! Dessalines! You were right after all!' – that James shows the great leader 'acknowledging his tragic failing not to have placed more trust in the black masses'.[21]

When Robeson was handed James's play, the actor had already read several scripts as part of a discussion with the Soviet film-maker Sergei Eisenstein about making a film on the Haiti revolution, although it is unclear whether or to what extent James knew about this. A mutual friend of James's and Robeson's had given the play to the Stage Society, a leading non-commercial play producing company, though now past its heyday. James recalled that the Society agreed to present the play if he could persuade Robeson to play the lead, but it took some time for him to track Robeson down. When he did, Robeson accepted on the spot. *Toussaint Louverture* received two performances in March 1936 at the Westminster Theatre, then boasting a modern profile through its association with the experimental Group Theatre. The play's director was Peter Godfrey (white), who, with his wife Molly Veness, had founded and run the pioneering Gate Theatre, where he had directed the first British production of *All God's Chillun Got Wings* in 1926 and his own burlesque version of *Uncle Tom's Cabin* in 1933 (both with white actors).

Among the diasporic members of the cast were a number who had appeared in *Stevedore*: Robert Adams, John Ahuma, Lawrence Brown, Rufus E. Fennell, Charles Johnson and Orlando Martins. Fennell and Johnson had been in *Basalik*, as had Frank Kennedy. Casting a large number of black parts was becoming easier, even if the skills levels remained drastically inconsistent. James later wrote of Godfrey's absences and having to rehearse the cast himself. He came under pressure to make cuts, not least from Robeson, but remembers a good collaboration with him. James later freely admitted that he lacked 'the instinct of the playwright', and several critics agreed.[22] *The Times* critic, who found the play 'continuously interesting' but 'informative rather than suggestive', complained of its 'woodenness'.[23] The *Sketch* wished the dialogue had been less prosaic and more poetic, but found Toussaint a 'real tragedy hero'.[24] Another critic wrote that *Toussaint Louverture* exposed audiences to a great black hero who 'emerges as a man of greater capacity and honour than the white men who contrived his downfall'.[25] Or, as the *New Leader* noted:

> The whole play cogently puts the problem of empire with its exploitation and slavery of the coloured people. The 'civilising' missions of the Capitalist Governments, their promises solemnly made and lightly scrapped, their trickery, makes a pretty picture for an audience whose rulers have the largest empire in the world under their domination. The production with its minimum of scenery, is excellently done by Peter Godfrey, and the large cast, many of them Negroes, succeeds in convincing the audience that an Empire is nothing of which any white civilisation can be proud.[26]

Robeson, as was often the case, fared better than the play, which had no further immediate life, despite its warm reception. The *New York Times* reported: 'although unevenly written and produced, [the drama] nevertheless held an appreciative audience's attention throughout, receiving an ovation at the final curtain.'[27]

The production came against the backdrop of the Italian invasion of Ethiopia in October 1935, an event which became a rallying cause for the Pan-Africanists in Britain and possibly led to tension between James and Robeson over the role and direction of the Soviet Union under Stalin. James, by now a Trotskyist, was openly critical of Soviet lack of support and its selling oil to fascist Italy, news of which caused a major break for many black activists with Stalinism. Robeson, whatever his private thoughts, was steadfastly pro-Soviet in public. It is not clear what or how many attempts were made to transfer the production, remount the play or have it published, but, although James does not record any disagreement with Robeson over Ethiopia, this political difference may have contributed to the play's demise.[28]

Padmore recommended the play's publication and performance in the US but without success. The Eisenstein project collapsed, as did another involving the team responsible for the 1936 *Show Boat* film featuring Robeson, who were pursuing a similar idea using the James script. The original playtext itself appeared to be lost, and most subsequent critical comment focused on James's book, *The Black Jacobins*, especially as James did not continue his playwriting. In the 1960s, with help from fellow Trinidadian Dexter Lyndersay, James reworked the play under the new title of *The Black Jacobins*. It had its première under Lyndersay's direction at the University of Ibadan in 1967 and was published in 1976. Fifty years after the first production, this new version was chosen by Yvonne Brewster to launch the London-based diasporic company Talawa.

In 2005, Christian Hogsbjerg, a PhD student, discovered the original text during his research on James. In his introduction to this text, he says the later play, *The Black Jacobins*, follows the same chronological structure as *Toussaint Louverture*, and contains many scenes built around incidents depicted in the earlier play. There is the same humour, the lively music and drumming ebbing and flowing into the action on stage, and there are still moments of rare dramatic power. Yet, Hogsbjerg believes, 'the richness of character that defines *Toussaint Louverture* is absent from the later play'. Hogsbjerg says James made three major modifications. While still a Greek chorus, the ordinary slaves are given greater emphasis, and James seems more conscious of the role and experience of women during the Revolution. The most striking difference, however, lies in the role of the individual in history. The later play ends not with Dessalines the heroic leader of the Haitian people, but with Dessalines the corrupt despot who betrayed Toussaint to the French. By the time of the rewriting, James had felt both the thrill and the frustration of colonial liberation. 'If *Toussaint Louverture* was about the vindication of national liberation struggles written in the age of colonialism', says Hogsbjerg, 'in *The Black Jacobins*, James and Lyndersay were trying to explore what lessons the Haitian Revolution might hold for national liberation struggles in the age of decolonisation'.[29]

Following *Toussaint Louverture*, the only play in which Robeson appeared that was written by a diasporic writer, he returned to the American left-wing repertoire for his next British stage appearance. This came in 1938 when he rejected a lucrative offer to appear in the West End, preferring instead to perform at the Communist-affiliated, amateur Unity Theatre in Ben Bengal's *Plant in the Sun*, a play about a sit-down strike in a New York sweet factory called to defend a colleague who has been sacked for organising the union. (Robeson played a white part to demonstrate Unity's rejection of surface naturalism.) Robeson sang at the official opening of Unity's own theatre, and was a tutor at Unity's theatre school as well as a member of its general council. For Robeson, Unity offered a political context, which had been lacking with the James play. Robeson's career in the US, where he returned when war broke out, meant he did not return to Unity as an actor. The links remained firm, however, until his death.

Although diapsoric actors were not involved in running Unity, its self-management system was an inspiration to them, and Unity continued to produce plays on anti-colonial and race issues after Robeson had left. It had planned to present Robeson again, in *Colony*, but, despite his absence, went ahead with the play in 1939 alongside *After the Tempest* in a double bill on imperialism. Both plays, by Geoffrey Trease (a white Englishman), are set on fictional islands, but in *Colony* the island is clearly recognisable as Jamaica, where sugar workers are striking for fair wages, better conditions and the right to organise in a trade union. There were several diasporic actors in the cast, including Robert Adams and Orlando Martins, who alternated the part written for Robeson of the strike leader, an impressive figure reminiscent of Alexander Bustamante, who in 1943 founded the Jamaican Labour Party. Under strong encouragement from the American Group Theatre, Unity decided to form a professional company and planned to revive *Colony* in the West End as its inaugural production, hopefully with Robeson, but the declaration of war interrupted the scheme. Unity, nevertheless, kept operating throughout the war and included in its 1943 repertoire *India Speaks* (also known as *Map of India*), a Living Newspaper in poem-form dealing with the famine in eastern India written by Mulk Raj Anand and including several Indians in the cast. Unity took the play to London's East End for a special showing to Indian seamen, and to Birmingham, Leeds and Cardiff as part of the India League's campaign on the famine and the need for Indian independence. Anand went on to write a similar Living Newspaper, *Famine*, for the Army Bureau of Current Affairs Play Unit, which was heavily influenced by people associated with Unity. When Unity finally launched a professional company in 1946, its artistic director Ted Willis invited Robert Adams to lead the opening show, *All God's Chillun Got Wings*, with the Cheshire-born Ida Shepley playing his sister. (As the company did not employ any more diasporic actors, white actors blacked up alongside them, although Robeson had not whited up in his earlier role at Unity.) Unity continued to be a home for diasporic actors in the post-war years in plays such as *Dragnet* (1947) by Joe MacColum and *Longitude 49* (1950) by Herb Tank, and several of these actors were seminal to the development of diasporic theatre in Britain, such as Yemi Ajibade, Mark Heath, Errol Hill, Errol John, Carmen Munroe, Anton Phillips, Frank Singuineau, and Rudolph Walker.

In *All God's Chillun Got Wings*, Adams and Shepley were reprising the roles they had played in a Negro Repertory Theatre production two years before, a production which probably represents the first attempt to establish a diasporic theatre company in Britain. Robeson had proposed the idea, as had the League of Coloured Peoples at Adams's suggestion (he was a founder member), but nothing came of it until Adams revived the notion during the war. Born in British Guiana, Adams trained as a teacher and acted in and directed amateur drama before coming to Britain in the late 1920s in order to be a professional actor. Like Orlando Martins, he had to take a series of poorly-paid jobs and was persuaded to take up wrestling, in which pursuit he earned minor celebrity as 'The Black Eagle', winning the heavyweight championship of the British

Empire. As well as appearing in *Stevedore*, *Toussaint Louverture* and *Colony*, Adams made West End appearances too, and in 1938 played the title part in O'Neill's *The Emperor Jones* at the Arts Theatre, Cambridge, the same year the BBC broadcast him in this role, the first black actor to appear as a leading character on British television.[30] In 1943, with help from a Unity activist Peter Noble, Adams began planning a black company that would stage ballet and dance as well as plays by black playwrights and, in association with the British Council, would tour the US and countries within the British Empire. The London Negro Repertory Theatre (aka Negro Repertory Theatre) was due to open in December 1943 at the Arts Theatre in a production of *All God's Chillun Got Wings* featuring Adams directed by André van Gyseghem, but there is no record of this occurring. Noble later recalled only one production by the company, in late 1944 of the same play but at Colchester Repertory Theatre.[31] Adams, who had become President of the Society for the Prevention of Racial Discrimination in Britain, directed and played the lead alongside the black actors George Browne, Earl Cameron, Martins and Shepley. Cameron remembers that Adams did not direct very well, and that Robert Digby, Colchester's director, had to take over.[32] Apparently Adams left in shame but was coaxed back, yet it represented a blow to the future prospects of the group, which did not survive. Adams, however, did not give up the idea of the group immediately. In 1946 Noble reports him announcing his intention, 'as soon as conditions permitted', of forming a Negro Theatre as part of the struggle for the 'artistic and social recognition for the negro race'.[33] One obstacle had been the lack of actors, says Noble, but this was no longer the case. Another barrier had been lack of plays, yet Noble lists a planned repertoire: *The Emperor Jones*, *All God's Chillun Got Wings* and a new play by Adams on a slave revolt in the Caribbean. (He is said to have written plays but none survives.) Other productions, it was hoped, would include James's *Toussaint Louverture*, Richard Wright's *Native Son*, and *Porgy and Bess*.

Unfortunately, these plans did not materialise, although Adams did play Bigger Thomas in *Native Son* in an adaptation by Paul Green and Wright in 1948 at a small club theatre in London. Through his appearances on TV, film, radio and stage, Adams was probably Britain's leading black actor, but tired and disillusioned, he took up the law and then returned to British Guiana where he became a head-teacher prior to his death in 1965.[34] Before he left acting, he wrote an article on the struggle black actors faced in Britain, and attacked the theatre industry bias in favour of Americans, a subject he spoke about at an Equity meeting at the time. Adams writes that when he arrived in Britain, he found the conception that 'only the American Negro artist had any talent. The African or West Indian was called second-rate'.[35] The problem was most pressing in 'the serious theatre' where the 'British Negro artist' is told either 'he [sic] has not the talent or that he will not be "box office"'. As a result, the 'Negro artist is still considered not an artist in his own right but as something contributory to the support of the white artists [...] However good he or she may be, the association must be with white artists and in a supplementary rather than a complementary role'. In the face of this, 'We British Negro artists claim respect for our individuality, and for the assessment of our contribution on its merit value'. Adams calls for government and Equity action, and for 'British Negroes' to use trade unionism to overcome the difficulties he outlines. He ends with a wider challenge to the British public and its institutions, a challenge that offers a prophetic statement of the value of the future theatre he did not live to see but helped to create:

> Recognise us artistically as equals, give us the opportunity to contribute as equals. Ours will be a dynamic contribution.

It was not until the last quarter of the twentieth century that an autonomous British diasporic theatre was established, though it was still not accepted as equal. Nevertheless, its roots can be traced directly back to the transitional achievements of the 1930s and 1940s, piecemeal, uneven and marginalised as they were. Through Robeson and a growing group of British diasporic actors, such as Orlando Martins and Robert Adams, the diasporic body was beginning to open up spaces to challenge dominant perceptions and enact its own agenda. In an era of blacking up and generally racist stereotyping that persisted for several more decades, it represented a significant accomplishment. This diasporic presence, however strained and insecure, was supported by a network of social and cultural organisations, which allowed the interplay between individual and collective to develop diasporic theatre as a validation of wider values transcending personal attainment. Critically, the construction of diasporic identity was being wrested from the colonising culture, particularly through the contribution of diasporic writers such as Una Marson and C.L.R. James. Although a diasporic centre was not formed, and a diasporic company enjoyed only a brief existence, the possibility of both had been affirmed in public. Their realisation, and the continuation of a broken tradition from this period, remained an aspiration for subsequent generations who were eventually able to turn ambition into reality.

Notes

1   See, for example Dominic Shellard, ed., *British Theatre Since the War* (New Haven and London: Yale University Press, 1999); Clive Barker and Maggie B. Gale, eds, *British Theatre Between the Wars, 1918–1939* (Cambridge: Cambridge University Press, 2000); Richard Eyre and

Nicholas Wright, *Changing Stages: A View of British Theatre in the Twentieth Century* (London: Bloomsbury, 2000); Michael Billington, *State of the Nation: British Theatre Since 1945* (London: Faber, 2007).

2   A further complication was language itself. Own-language theatre groups in Britain using Hindi, Gujarati, Marathi or Urdu, for example, were important in the post-war years for community cohesion and identity but in the 1970s Tara Arts saw this trend as conservative and, instead, used English as a sign of modernity and assertion of equality. Later, as Tara developed its own aesthetic, it used a mix of English and Asian languages. With African and Caribbean groups and writers (where English was the common language), the challenge was to use Creole or dialect as equally valid as standard English.

3   Herbert Marshall and Mildred Stock's pioneering biography *Ira Aldridge: The Negro Tragedian* (London: Rockliff, 1958) was an isolated case and not widely known in Britain. In 1989, my book *The Story of Unity Theatre* (London: Lawrence and Wishart, 1989) identified the black contribution to Unity Theatre and noted the beginnings of a black theatre history. The growing field includes: Susan Croft, 'Black Women Playwrights in Britain', in Trevor R. Griffiths and Margaret Llewellyn-Jones, eds, *British and Irish Women Dramatists Since 1958: A Critical Handbook* (Buckingham: Open University, 1993); Stephen Bourne, *Black in the British Frame: Black People in British Film and Television 1896–1996* (London: Cassell, 1998); Jeffrey Green, *Black Edwardians: Black People in Britain 1901–1914* (London: Frank Cass, 1998); Gabrielle Griffin, *Contemporary Black and Asian Women Playwrights in Britain* (Cambridge: Cambridge University Press, 2003); Geoffrey V. Davis and Anne Fuchs, eds, *Staging New Britain: Aspects of Black and South Asian British Theatre Practice* (Brussels: PIE-Peter Lang, 2006); Dimple Godiwala, ed., *Alternatives Within the Mainstream: British Black and Asian Theatres* (Newcastle: Cambridge Scholars Press, 2006). The University of Exeter won grant money for a four-year project on British South-Asian Theatre that resulted in a conference in 2008 and promises two (forthcoming) volumes.

4   The research for this essay forms part of the wider research undertaken for a forthcoming book for Routledge on the history of British diasporic theatre which draws on a great deal of scholarly work on the periods from the medieval onward as well as those publications mentioned in footnote 1.

5   The Indian Art and Dramatic Society appeared under the auspices of the Union of East and West, the aim of which, according to a 1920 edition of the play *Sakuntala* prepared for the English stage by the IADS and Union founder Kedar Nath Das Gupta, was 'to establish a meeting for the East and the West in the field of Art, Philosophy, Literature, Music and the Drama'. For a more detailed account of the IADS and Indian Players, see my essay 'Images on Stage: A Historical Survey before 1975', in Graham Ley and Sarah Dadswell, eds, *Critical Essays on British South Asian Theatre* (Exeter: University of Exeter Press, forthcoming).

6   *The Times*, 7 June 1922.

7   *The Keys* 1.3, January 1934, p. 43.

8   Delia Jarrett-Macauley, *The Life of Una Marson: 1905–65* (Manchester: Manchester University Press, 1998), p. vii.

9   Jarrett-Macauley, p. 43.

10 See *The Negro Worker* 2.5 (February–March 1935), p. 2 for the refusal to present a benefit concert.

11 Marie Seton, 'English Theatre of the Left', *New Theatre* (December 1934), p. 21.

12 George W. Bishop, *Hampstead and St John's Wood Advertiser*, 15 November 1934.

13 Paul Peters and George Sklar, *Stevedore* (London: Jonathan Cape, 1935), p. 123.

14 Peters and Sklar, p. 137.

15 *Basalik* was written for Robeson by a white American, Norma Leslie Munro, under the name Peter Garland.
16 Louverture is also spelled L'Ouverture but the first spelling is both the one the Haitian leader himself adopted and the one used by James in the original playtext.
17 Date of conception from author's note in the original 1936 programme of *Toussaint Louverture*, quoted by Christian Hogsbjerg in his Introduction to C.L.R. James, *Toussaint Louverture: The Story of the Only Successful Slave Revolt in History* (Durham: Duke University Press, forthcoming) to which I am indebted and from which the play's quotations are taken.
18 The fact that James could use the terms 'black' and 'negro' at the same time underlines the terminological complexity referred to elsewhere in the essay.
19 Hogsbjerg, Introduction.
20 Hogsbjerg, Introduction.
21 Hogsbjerg, Introduction.
22 Paul Buhle, *C.L.R. James: The Artist as Revolutionary* (London: Verso, 1988), p. 22.
23 Charles Darwin, *The Times*, 17 March 1936.
24 Ivor Brown, *The Sketch*, 25 March 1936.
25 W.A. Darlington, *Daily Telegraph*, 17 March 1936. Quoted in Sheila Tully Boyle and Andrew Bunie, *Paul Robeson: The Years of Promise and Achievement* (Amherst: University of Massachusetts Press, 2001), p. 342.
26 *New Leader*, 20 March 1936.
27 *New York Times*, 16 March 1936.
28 One scene, Act II, Scene 1, was published in the British journal *Life and Letters Today* (Spring 1936). Buhle (p. 57) says political differences between Robeson and James did affect the future of the play but offers no evidence. Hogsbjerg, however, quotes James later remembering that in the context of the rising Stalinist terror against Trotskyists, though he and Robeson never quarrelled, 'the idea of doing the play automatically faded into nothing'. Hogsbjerg, Introduction.
29 Hogsbjerg, Introduction.
30 See Stephen Bourne, *Black in the British Frame: The Black Experience in British Film and Television* (London: Continuum, 2001), pp. 72–6, for more on Adams's screen career.
31 See Colin Chambers, *The Story of Unity Theatre*, p. 187, fn 19.
32 Earl Cameron, Blackgrounds interview, 29 May 1997, part of a series of interviews held in the Theatre Collection of the Victoria & Albert Museum, London.
33 'Why Not a Negro Theatre?', in Peter Noble, ed., *British Theatre* (London: British Yearbook, 1946), pp. 61–3. Noble also refers to the group in his book *The Negro in Films* (London: Skelton Robinson, 1948), pp. 173–8.
34 Adams did not entirely give up acting but made only a brief return to the stage in Britain, in 1958 in Eugene O'Neill's *The Iceman Cometh*, and he made a number of minor television and film appearances.
35 'Problems of the Negro in the Theatre', *New Theatre* 4.5 (November 1947), p. 11.

Adapting to the Conjuncture: Walter Greenwood, History and *Love on the Dole*

Ben Harker

Published in a decade when working-class fiction became a significant presence on the cultural landscape in Britain, Walter Greenwood's *Love on the Dole* (1933) has enjoyed a semi-canonical afterlife not shared by novels written by contemporaries such as Harold Heslop, Walter Brierley and Lewis Jones. Whereas the texts produced by those writers soon became what one critic calls 'the exotic fragments of a long forgotten culture' – a culture excavated and reconstructed by leftist intellectuals and publishers amidst the political and ideological struggles of the 1970s and 1980s – Greenwood's most famous novel has never slipped from view.[1] Consistently in print since its first publication in 1933, *Love on the Dole* was to become *the* working-class novel of the early 1930s, frequently selected to stand in for a body of fiction of which it was originally only a part.

The endurance of *Love on the Dole* was never inevitable and, as Raymond Williams notes, the processes through which selective traditions are established, consolidated and renewed are historically complex, involving institutions (cultural, educational, political, economic) and formations – 'movements and tendencies, in intellectual and artistic life'.[2] Critics have often detected in Greenwood's novel liberal assumptions and conservative formal devices, and suggested that *Love on the Dole*'s upbeat 1930s reception and subsequent success is directly related to its tendency to mediate working-class thought and feeling in ways acceptable to a middle-class readership.[3] This article attempts to refine and develop questions around the novel's ongoing cultural presence. Arguing that the novel's success cannot be retrospectively reduced to – or read off from – conservative textual inscriptions alone, I recover the cultural process of the novel's long launch in the period between the original publication (1933) and its cinema adaptation by John Baxter for British National (1941). It was in this period, I argue, that the novel was first elevated from its position as just another regional 'proletarian novel' and established as a widely circulated narrative seen to encapsulate depression-era working-class suffering. I argue that the process of cultural projection, in which the novel was transposed from page to screen via the institutions of repertory theatre and the West End stage – a process which also kept the novel in print and created new readers for it – was enabled by a productive interplay between the novel's political ambivalence or openness and the author's willingness and ability to adapt and ideologically re-code the text not only across different media and their conventions, but also across changing times. As the article's title suggests, Greenwood, like his text, proved adaptable; he was not a proletarian dupe fleeced of his work by an unscrupulous culture industry, but an emerging professional writer actively participating in the re-articulation of his text.

I

Set in working-class Salford during a period of deepening economic crisis, Greenwood's debut novel was published in June 1933, drew praise from reviewers across the political spectrum and was reprinted four times over the next two years.[4] The novel's instant commercial success and critical acclaim, however, have subsequently been counterbalanced by criticism from the left focusing on the text's tendency to do the hegemonic work of naturalising economic and political structures. According to this line of thought the novel's critique is compromised by its refusal to represent directly the exploiting class, a refusal read as symptomatic of an inability to grasp the totality of social relations or the interdependent nature of social classes. The novel has also been criticised for leaving out sustained and explicit coverage of oppositional working-class collective agency, be it the General Strike of 1926, political advances for the Labour Party in the 1929 General Election, or the activities of the Communist Party and its front organisations such as the National Unemployed Workers' Movement (NUWM).[5] But although the novel's overriding mood is indeed one of pessimism and stasis – readers have often observed that it ends as it begins, a narrative device that underscores a theme of incarceration within apparently unassailable class structures – these criticisms run the risk of what Raymond Williams calls 'reducing works to finished products and activities to fixed positions', underplaying the text's own vexed and ambivalent location as the site of Walter Greenwood's active and conflicted struggle for a coherent political analysis of contemporary events.[6]

The novel was written in 1932 by a self-educated working-class intellectual committed to the Labour Party; it both reports on and refracts within its pessimistic plot structure the political crisis of the early 1930s in which the second Labour government collapsed, and in which social classes became detached from traditional party loyalties as the National Government was formed to shore up systemic economic failure. Greenwood's novel castigates the National Government for its socially divisive policies, but the text is less the source of coherent political analysis than a search for it.[7] Deeply marked by ideological uncertainty, *Love on the Dole* is pulled between radicalism and defeatism, or between a belief that socialist critique and political engagement can bring significant change, and crisis-ridden doubts around the effectiveness of such interventions. That Greenwood became stuck when struggling to draw the plot to a satisfactory closure was as much an ideological as an artistic problem, an instance of political options appearing to be blocked.[8] Indeed, ideological instability is inscribed into the novel even before it begins: the first edition was launched with an eye-catching page of epigraphs sampling radical voices including Rosa Luxemburg's assessment that contemporary society is in the midst of 'a new collapse, a fresh gigantic overthrow'. Perhaps recognising that his finished text did not match these revolutionary inscriptions, Greenwood cut the epigraphs from the second edition.[9]

II

Love on the Dole's central plotlines illustrate the contradiction implied by its title – that human instincts such as love are incompatible with de-humanising life on the dole – and does so by narrating the thwarted rites of passage of brother and sister Harry and Sally Hardcastle. Harry serves his engineering apprenticeship but finds himself unemployed and unable to afford to marry his pregnant fiancée; his sister, mill-hand Sally Hardcastle, succumbs to the predatory sexual advances of local bookmaker Sam Grundy after her fiancé, the autodidact intellectual and Labour Party activist Larry Meath, dies after being beaten by the police on a political demonstration.

On one hand the fact that Greenwood's plotting fatally punishes the text's ideologue Larry Meath for his political activism reinforces a sense of the futility of organised resistance;[10] on the other, the novel's negative line on political commitments is checked by its sporadic but insistent didacticism. The text repeatedly disrupts its own narrative flow by creating space for Meath to present political lessons to his fellow Salfordians and to Greenwood's readers, teaching sessions which exceed the requirements of plot development and extend a working-class literary tradition of the socialist autodidactic as authorial mouthpiece famously inaugurated with the character of Frank Owen in Robert Tressell's *The Ragged Trousered Philanthopists* (1914).[11] These sessions are also reminiscent of the didactic interruptions of Brechtian theatre which, in the words of Walter Benjamin, 'brings the action to a standstill in midcourse and thereby compels the spectator to take up a position towards the action'.[12] Meath's interruptions resonate through the novel on themes from the spirit-crushing ugliness of industrialised society to the inherently exploitative economics of capitalism illustrated through lessons based on Marx's labour theory of value.[13] And though the novel's ending – Meath's death and Sally selling herself to Grundy – might be read as the text retreating from political concerns to private tragedy, Sally's fall also quietly reactivates Meath's teaching, tentatively edging the text towards a more challenging critique – overlooked by critics – which it implies but cannot fully articulate (an instance of what Williams calls 'the finite but significant openness' of the text to 'many actual initiatives and contributions').[14] Greenwood might not represent the exploiting class in action, but Meath's teachings indelibly fix into the text the idea that all workers are reduced to commodities under capitalist relations of production and have no choice but to sell their labour to the highest bidder. Though Greenwood pulls back from making the link explicitly, the novel's ending is powerful in part because Sally breaches conventional morality and pushes that lesson to its grotesque limit, skilfully managing the commodification of her body and using her new influence to secure work for her brother and father. In *History and Class Consciousness* (1922), Georg Lukács argued that the process of the worker recognising his or her status as a commodity loosened the commodity form's hold, moving working-class consciousness in a critical direction towards the understanding of a reified social totality.[15] Sally's insight into her own commodity status is geared instead towards individual survival: she withdraws her labour from the mill and takes it in-house, splitting herself between the business woman who manages her only commodity and the worker who does the work. This moral outrage – the labour of prostitution – enables her to secure a social promotion unavailable by any other means.

III

Love on the Dole's combination of realistic conventions, dispersed political readings and commercial success made it unlikely adaptation material for early 1930s leftist theatre groups such as the Communist-dominated Workers' Theatre Movement, which favoured highly stylised agitprop modes to carry the message. But these very properties raised the possibility of the novel's more mainstream stage adaptation.[16] Within months of publication Manchester-based playwright Ronald Gow, fresh from West End success with *Gallows Glorious* (1933), a play celebrating the American slave-liberator John Brown, had begun collaborating with Greenwood on the text. (Gow later recalled being struck that 'a play of protest might be written about a contemporary evil, rather than slavery'.)[17] Jointly credited to Gow and Greenwood, the play *Love on the Dole* opened at the Manchester Repertory Theatre, Rusholme, on 26 February 1934. Positive reviews and sell-out shows led to the play's scheduled fortnight run being extended to four weeks.[18] This initial success provided the foundation for a tour of the North and the Midlands on which, according to newspaper estimates, the play's total audience reached 800,000.[19] The tour's success in turn created momentum for a London transfer, and on 30 January

1935 the play opened at the West End's Garrick Theatre where the premiere was attended by prominent Labour Party figures including Lord Ponsonby, Lady Cripps and the recently elected London County Council leader, Herbert Morrison.[20] Here the production ran for 391 performances, provoking discussions in the House of Commons and becoming a central cultural event in mid-1930s London.[21] When, in *The Road to Wigan Pier* (1937), George Orwell cited *Love on the Dole* for yielding real insight into lives of the North's unemployed, he was referring not to the novel but to the stage version, which he assumed his readers had seen.[22]

The process of critically reconstructing the novel's theatrical adaptation, and of considering how its political meanings and arguments were dramatised and contained in production, is hampered by the absence of recordings or photographs, but assisted by the play's history in print. It was published twice in the mid-1930s: the Jonathan Cape edition of 1935 was prepared for publication prior to the London transfer, and reprints the text used for the Manchester performances and subsequent tour; the Samuel French acting edition of 1936 reprints the text as performed in London.[23] What emerges in comparing the two is that the original Manchester adaptation underwent significant further revision *en route* to the West End, and that *Love on the Dole* was adapted for the stage not once but twice.

The character of Meath is at the core of the novel's tempered radicalism, and what happens to his didactic voice – a master-code surrounding and focusing the novel's events – is necessarily central to the political tenor of its stage adaptation. At the Manchester Repertory Theatre, where *Love on the Dole* stood out amongst an otherwise standard season of thrillers and historical dramas (the theatre's publicity materials played down radical associations by reassuring regular customers that this was 'true drama "Galsworthy" style' with 'glimpses of light' and 'a streak of real Lancashire humour') the production gave airtime to Meath's interruptions, whilst also muffling their resonances and meanings.[24] The stage set recreated the kitchen living-room of the Hardcastle home at the front of the stage with the street running behind; Act One Scene One begins with Meath audibly teaching on the street while Sal, indoors, listens through an open door.[25] With politics in the street's background, the domestic scene in the foreground, and the view through the door blocked by a persistent heckler, the tableau gives a clue to the production's commercially attuned, plot-driven priorities. And whereas in the novel Greenwood maximises the impact of Meath's teaching by carefully tailoring each lesson to its context – Meath talks about the de-humanising effects of brutal surroundings in his evening meetings held in slum streets and the labour theory of value during breaks from labour in the engineering works – the adaptation compresses Meath's lessons into just one short session, jumbling together a number of his main themes.[26] Meath's arguments are further obscured by the heckling to which – unlike in the equivalent scene in the novel – he soon gives ground, retreating indoors to his private life with Sally Hardcastle.

This process of sidelining didacticism is intensified for the London transfer where a revised stage direction now dictates that the political lesson must be inaudible to the audience:

> out of sight and almost out of hearing, a SPEAKER is addressing a meeting. We cannot hear his words, but Sally can, and it is interesting to note what he says. The angry voice of the SPEAKER, accompanied by the noise of the CROWD, suggests the troubled background of the lives of these people.[27]

So whilst the Manchester production muffled Meath's, and the novel's, central political lesson – nobody who saw the original production at the Manchester Repertory Theatre would have emerged from the auditorium understanding Marx's labour theory of value – the London production excised it altogether, translating the critique of the commodity form presented by a working-class intellectual into the turbulent noise of a troubled crowd. The effect of marginalising and editing Meath's teaching not only removes didactic impediments or interruptions to the plot's flow, but also dismantles the novel's critical framework, assigning a more passive role to the audience. As noted above, like the audience of epic theatre, the reader of the novel is required to 'take up a position towards the action', actively producing a dialogue between Meath's teaching and the narrative's events (characters in the novel enact a similar process: Mrs Bull cites one of Meath's lessons to explain the economics of rent and profit).[28] Significantly in the first adaptation and more forcefully in the second, the novel's hesitant radicalism is edited away, and illusionism and plot-driven conventions are observed in productions that closely reflect what Raymond Williams describes as the accommodation of theatrical naturalism's once challenging conventions to 'the norms of the orthodox culture'.[29] Environment here is shown to shape human nature, which is therefore 'socially and culturally specific' (the 'real environment' produced on-stage reflects that environment is 'one of the true agencies of action'); but the broader economic, social and political structures and crises that in turn shape that environment are present only as 'reports from elsewhere' or 'things seen from the window or as shouts from the street'; didacticism is altogether eschewed.[30] Through these conventions, audience attention is re-directed from dialogic engagement with social, political and structural questions and hidden social forces – capitalism, surplus value, the commodity form – to the realm of the personal and moral within a given environment. Sally's fall, when it eventually comes in Act Three, now plays out as a family tragedy in which a decent working-class character falls into amorality rather than, as in the novel, a blurred but nonetheless grotesquely unsettling narration of alienated labour.

IV

In the novel Meath's Labour Party activism runs through the text: he appears in a variety of politicised contexts from street and works meetings to Labour Club rambles.[31] Though his political commitments come into conflict with the private concerns of his relationship with Sally, the two are by no means presented as incompatible or mutually exclusive. But as noted above, both stage versions open with Meath withdrawing from the public forum of class politics (more rapidly in London where the teaching scene is cut short), a retreat that succinctly pre-figures his trajectory in the play. In both versions he leaves the street to confess his disillusionment, admitting that 'ideals and politics' no longer 'seem to matter like [they] did' and that Sally has 'changed' him.[32] This more individualistic consciousness – in which his idealism is channelled from street to home and from collective politics to the sanctuary of personal relationships – is fed by a creeping conviction that a political 'fresh start' is almost unimaginable when working-class people are so mired in the false consciousness induced by 'daft Irish sweeps and their coupons and their betting'.[33] Both adaptations rework one of the novel's central tropes – that of a potential working-class political awakening – to substantiate this re-casting of Meath from organic intellectual, with optimism of the will, to lapsed idealist now finding an alternative space in the consolations of private life. In the novel political awakening signifies a new horizon for Meath and his class, as when he implores his audience to 'awaken to the fact that Society has the means, the skill, and the knowledge to afford us the opportunity to become Men and Women in the fullest sense of those terms'.[34] In the play this vision is assigned a more negative meaning. As he explains to Sally:

> You know, you can call those men stupid if you like, but you can't help but admire their loyalty. I mean their loyalty to a system that's made 'em what they are [...] Or are they just asleep? Gad, that's what I'm afraid of! Wakening up suddenly to find they've been done. When people wake up all of a sudden they don't act very reasonably.[35]

From projecting the fresh start from which the working class could reach towards a better future of deepened humanity, political intervention is recast as managing Hanky Park's rude awakening from a sleepwalking false consciousness into a fallen world of alienation. From a conduit for political transformation, albeit one which seeks to resist more impatient communist political currents in the interest of gradualism, Meath on-stage becomes a mediator between capital and labour, or between established structures (the economy, the city council, the police) and the blind instincts of a potentially destructive working class. Recast from vision-inspired political activist to a world-weary stabiliser of the status quo, any sense of his eventual death as a collective, political loss for the community whose interests he represents is duly reduced. Unlike in the novel, where Meath continues to embody political hope throughout, in the stage production his tragedy becomes essentially a private affair cruelly mocking Sally's conviction that 'they can't tek away our love'.[36]

V

The adaptations' handling of law, order and the state is another key site in their complex political mediations. Both adaptations compress and sharpen the tangled novelistic plot by cutting away secondary characters, in particular Ned Narkey, a heavy drinking First World War veteran who has no time for a 'white livered conchie' like Meath, his rival for Sally Hardcastle's affections.[37] In the novel Narkey weathers the depression by joining the police force, where he settles old scores, energetically wielding his truncheon during the demonstration against the Means Test on which his old adversary Meath is seriously injured.[38] As a result, Meath's death in the novel is only partly a political matter; in line with the text's ambivalent political readings, the episode hovers ambiguously between an instance of police brutality and more personal plotting (the vengefulness of a rival suitor). His drawn-out death has a similar effect: injured on the demonstration, he dies later in hospital where his longstanding consumption contributes to a decline triggered but not wholly caused by state repression.

Paradoxically, the plot-driven adaptation of the novel for the stage generates political overtones that conflict with the countervailing de-radicalising thrust. In the streamlined play Meath is now unambiguously truncheoned to death by the police and dies promptly on the scene even though 'he was trying to turn men back' from direct confrontation.[39] As in the novel, the plotting still enacts a symbolic punishment for those ideological tendencies that in the adaptation frequently blind Meath to the truth;[40] at the same time, at least in the original adaptation for the Manchester production, Meath's death is now used to develop a new, cautionary critical discourse around the state and repression. Act Two Scene One, which has no equivalent in Greenwood's novel and was cut from the London show, introduces a representative, unnamed policeman who is smugly ignorant and casually authoritarian, if not proto-fascistic. Boasting that he is more interested in football than in the break up of the League of Nations, he explains that he sees life as it is, and compares people in Hanky Park to 'maggots squirming in a tin [...] wriggling an' fightin', an' none on 'em knows how they got in, nor how they're goin' to get out'.[41] The inclusion of this view foregrounds the authoritarian tendencies of the police behind Meath's death, and lends some credence to the views of the rabble-rousing Communist – nicknamed 'Mr Trotski' [sic] by Harry Hardcastle senior – who claims that the police are 'Traitors to their class!', 'Enemies of the workers!' and the 'iron heel of a bourgeois aristocracy'.[42] Though the vernacular analysis of Mrs Bull, who describes one policeman as 'a blurry Mussoloni', is more typical of the play's idiom, the Manchester production repeatedly aligns the police with the political right.[43] In a twist to the stage adaptation's political toning-down, then, the first adaptation tentatively introduces into Greenwood's early 1930s novel the political concerns of an emerging mid-1930s popular front, identifying how proto- and pre- fascist tendencies might emerge from within establishment power structures in the context of spreading fascism abroad and deepening inequalities at home.[44]

Though Mrs Bull's Mussolini line remains, the London production otherwise retracts this implied political reading in an explicit ideological re-coding. The policeman's appearance in Act Two Scene One is cut and replaced by a knock-about comic scene involving a drunken man and his long-suffering wife, a switch which underscores the naturalist motif of Hanky Park's irresistible and brutalising determinism.[45] Though Meath is still killed by the police, the loss of this earlier scene shifts emphasis from Meath as a victim of 'the iron heel' towards Meath as tragically caught between his own public spiritedness, the strong arm of the law, and the dangerous energies of political extremism – energies that become significantly more extreme for the London production. In the Manchester production Meath argues with 'Mr Trotski', in London Meath is required physically to restrain the firebrand;[46] in Manchester demonstrators sing 'The Red Flag', the anthem of the historically moderate British Labour movement; in London they sing 'The Internationale', with its associations of the Paris Commune and international revolution.[47] And in Manchester the demonstration is shown to give voice to genuine community grievances around the Means Test, and expression to an intuitive mistrust of authority demonstrated by the low intensity insubordination of characters such as Mrs Jike, Mrs Bull and Mrs Dorbell. In the London re-write, however, collective self-organisation is predominantly figured as a dangerous flood rushing behind the domestic interior of the Hardcastle home, drawing Meath, Harry Hardcastle and Mr Hardcastle in its wake. And even though the political case for equating incipient fascism with the British establishment was much stronger in late January 1935 (when the production transferred to London) than twelve months earlier (when it had opened in Manchester) – this period had witnessed the rise of Oswald Mosley, the notorious support of the British Union of Fascists by Lord Rothermere's newspapers, and widespread concern that police had shown a bias towards the Blackshirts during the Olympia Rally in June 1934 – the revised text cut away the admittedly tentative anti-fascist readings introduced into the original stage adaptation to caution against extremism in all its manifestations.[48] The dominant line emerging from the London production is a running protest against the de-humanising conditions of Hanky Park, overlaid with the suggestion that ideological thought conflicts with personal happiness, radical self-organisation generates tragedy, and that politics is best left to others.

VII

The Manchester production's muffled critique of structural forces and hesitant articulation of popular front political arguments made it sufficiently distinct from the city's usual repertory programming to create a rallying point for those who argued that, in an era of talking movies and mass theatre closures, the mainstream dramatic arts had lost their nerve, giving ground to the narrow commercial concerns that governed the West End.[49] The more tempered London production, by contrast, had the paradoxical effect of affirming those commercial circuits. The 'West End' might easily be ridiculed as the domain of 'effete' audiences, 'cocktail comedies', and 'neo-Tudor villas', but in staging the play was showing a willingness to tackle the real issues facing the 'distressed areas'.[50] Furthermore, the production demonstrated London's cultural inclusiveness in welcoming an artefact direct from what George Orwell called that 'strange country' of the industrial north in the form of a show still rooted in the original Lancashire production.[51] Staged at a moment when calls for a National Theatre were augmented by a critical consensus that commercialism and artistic timidity had narrowed theatre's social concerns and audience base, *Love on the Dole* at the Garrick validated the economic, social and regional divisions implicit in the notion of a culturally central 'West End' in the act of appearing to unsettle such divisions.

Headlines such as 'London sees Lancashire' encapsulated the novelty of the eventual transfer.[52] This was not a southern re-reading of a northern play, but the real thing which appeared to eschew metropolitan mediation: some London critics even speculated that the production was so true to life that the cast might actually be 'out of work cotton operatives' playing themselves (all were professional actors).[53] According to a number of London critics, the fact that the production was embedded in the place where it was set combined with the immediate liveness of theatre to bring 'the mind of the spectator into contact with realities': some were moved to charity as a result, others came away feeling 'grateful for small mercies'.[54]

Greenwood himself attended the first night where his presence authorised the production. He was praised by London critics for the working-class authenticity which licensed him to speak (he'd been 'kicked around all his life'), for his steadfast commitment to the harsh realities of Salford (he told one reporter that he didn't want to stay in London and 'live soft'), and for his public-spirited political moderation (his constructive political activities as a recently elected Labour Councillor were widely reported).[55] Regional identity and biographical straightforwardness reinforced the sense that his play sidestepped sentimentality, melodrama and extreme ideology in favour of 'plain straightforward statement of fact'.[56] This was a view shared by Herbert Morrison, who applauded Greenwood as 'a man who can write Labour propaganda with a sense of humour', meaning perhaps that the play humorously foregrounded inequalities without advocating radical structural transformation or extra-parliamentary politics; after all, Greenwood's own social promotion from Salford to the West End was on hand to imply that the poverty trap could be sprung, and to affirm the fundamental rightness of a society whose hard times were movingly dramatised in his work.[57] The London production's highly mediated authenticity satisfied a liberal compulsion to face the facts, giving the impression of getting behind ideology to present directly a distant social reality whilst consistently constructing that reality in terms of dominant social logic. That logic was augmented by the illusionistic theatrical conventions which removed the novel's didactic impediments and, in Walter Benjamin's terms, reproduced rather than revealed social conditions.[58]

VIII

The West End success of *Love on the Dole* created an expanding market for the novel, and brought Greenwood to the attention of Britain's film industry: he was hired by Basil Dean's Ealing Studios to write the screenplay for the new picture starring his fellow Lancastrian George Formby. *No Limit* (1935), which involved a working-class character enjoying rapid social promotion through victory at the Isle of Man TT races, was a transposed autobiography in which the dizzy pace of Greenwood's own social mobility was recast in fictional form. (Greenwood would marry the American actress and heiress Pearl Alice Osgood in 1937, and relocate from Salford to Surrey.)

The film industry was not only drawn to Greenwood's talents but also to the novel that had made him – reprinted four times in 1935 – especially following the stage success of *Love on the Dole* (after London the play transferred to Paris and then New York, where Eleanor Roosevelt saw the show).[59] But whereas the Lord Chamberlain and the conventions of commercially oriented theatrical naturalism permitted the controlled catharsis of unhappy endings, 1930s film censorship more vigilantly managed the mass mediation of working-class social conditions to working-class people. Shaped by this context of censorship, films dealing in working-class life habitually constructed the real through a cluster of conventions combining humour, the chipper acceptance of circumstances by the characters, or personal, imaginary resolutions to structural inequalities.[60] The success of *No Limit* was a measure of Greenwood's professional adaptability: he adroitly created for Formby an on-screen working-class identity with which audiences could identify; he also de-contextualised that identity from class conflict, and resolved the narrative with Formby's individual success – the ideal fantasy fix to a class-ridden society.[61]

Even in its West End incarnation, however, *Love on the Dole* was another matter; though shorn of didacticism, its residual naturalist core was true to the novel in stubbornly insisting that material conditions are at some level constitutive, and that the freedom necessary for meaningful personal fulfilment is dependent upon basic conditions being met. The scenario remained structurally incompatible with hegemonic cinematic conventions, and plans for a film adaptation that might have brought *Love on the Dole* back into the type of place it described famously fell foul of the British Board of Film Censors in 1936. The general preoccupation with 'the tragic and sordid side of poverty', and the particular reactions to such poverty in the form of prostitution and violent political demonstration, made it a 'very undesirable' subject for a film.[62] Despite Greenwood's foothold in the film industry and his rapid mastery of its ways of seeing, a second appeal to film *Love on the Dole* was also rejected.[63]

IX

The political conjuncture would have to be redefined before the film could be made. Stuart Hall notes:

> What defines the 'conjunctural' – the immediate terrain of the struggle – is not simply the given economic conditions, but precisely the 'incessant and persistent' efforts which are being made to defend and conserve the position. If the crisis is deep – 'organic' – these efforts cannot merely be defensive. They will be *formative*: a new balance of forces, the emergence

of new elements, the attempt to put together a new 'historical bloc', new political configurations and philosophies, a profound restructuring of the state and the ideological discourses which construct the crisis and represent it as 'lived', as a practical reality; new programmes and policies, pointing to a new result, a new sort of 'settlement' – 'within certain limits'. These do not 'emerge': they have to be constructed. Political and ideological work is required to disarticulate old formations, and to rework their elements into new configurations.[64]

In the mid-1930s *Love on the Dole*'s cinema adaptation was blocked by its resistance to those socially stabilising cinematic conventions that required either consolatory narratives about existing conditions or imaginary resolutions which left structural inequalities untouched. The early war years, on the other hand, witnessed a shift from defensive to actively 'formative' hegemonic efforts with the widespread cultural circulation of discourses 'disarticulat[ing] old formations' and promising 'a new sort of "settlement"' in the form of the economic, political and social reconstruction considered necessary to secure popular consent to fight and win the war. This wartime '[p]olitical and ideological work' – the enunciation of a different social formation – supplied the resolution to the novel's milieu that the censors had required and that the text otherwise lacked. 'The Germans are fighting a revolutionary war for definite objectives', observed one prominent voice at the Ministry of Information in July 1940. 'We must put forward a positive and revolutionary aim admitting that the old order has collapsed and asking people to fight for a new order.'[65] Film director John Baxter saw his employing company British National as committed to projecting this new order in providing 'a glimpse of the better world we all envisage after these sacrifices and hardships are through'.[66] Teamed up with Greenwood, who eagerly embarked on a second collaboration to adapt his novel, Baxter created from *Love on the Dole* a semi-official propaganda picture aptly described as 'the opening shot of the People's War'.[67]

The 'old order' or sordid side of 1930s life – unrepresentable on screen in 1936 unless carefully managed – was good subject matter in 1941: it reminded cinema-goers that victory in the war would enable the past to be resolved by the process of post-war reconstruction that Greenwood supported. The film's action, set just ten years earlier, is now distanced, sealed into 'the darker pages of our industrial history' through a written preface.[68] Another scrolling text concludes the film, this time signed by wartime Labour minister A.V. Alexander. Eliding for rhetorical effect distinctions between the present and future, the articulation of a promise and its realisation, Alexander's text reassures viewers that the past is now settled, unemployment over and that the reward of those who have 'responded magnificently' to war 'must be a New Britain'.

The intervening film found a clarity of ideological purpose lacking in the novel's hesitant radicalism and the play's often commercially oriented mediations. 'If every man and woman in Britain could see this film', wrote one critic in June 1941, 'I don't think we would ever go back to the dreadful pre-war years when two million men and women were allowed to rot in idleness'.[69] Larry Meath's teachings and ideological convictions, sidelined during the mid-1930s stage adaptation, are modernised and re-centred to convey the message. Marxist arguments uncovering capitalism's inherently exploitative (and therefore, presumably, unreformable) underpinnings are substituted for the more conciliatory politics of settlement between capital and labour ('We don't set the blame on any one section of the community', says Meath in a newly written addition to his restored street-meeting speech). In the play political engagement is presented as an impediment to personal happiness; here Meath is reconceived as an ideologue of political truce and a prophet of post-war reconstruction; the political consciousness and collective visions he represents are now the pre-condition for a new start for all, in contrast to what Meath calls the 'every man for himself' mindset of discredited 1930s liberal capitalism. Ideologically recoded to express a people's war vision of a national family united in adversity and awaiting better times, the film rejects the play's cautionary equation of establishment structures and proto-fascism. The police are no longer embryonic Mussolinis, but the reasonable and organised representatives of a rational state who are justifiably forceful when faced with provocateurs bent on thwarting the common interest. Rather than bludgeoned by a police truncheon, Meath is now accidentally trampled to death by a police horse, tragically caught in crossfire between the upholders of the rule of law and those who would sabotage the process of constructive reform; his death creates what one critic aptly calls 'a martyr for the moderate constitutional socialism that might one day cooperate with the authorities for the common good'.[70] The novel closed as it began, ingraining a sense of futile repetition; the Manchester version of the play closed with a scene of pathos in which Mrs Hardcastle imagines a springtime which seems never to arrive in Hanky Park. In the film spring becomes the post-war settlement invoked in its panoramic conclusion. The cyclical pattern is broken and the future enters the scene as Mrs Hardcastle steps out of character to imagine a world where 'we'll all be wanted', a desire symbolically fulfilled by the ascending arc of the camera which rises to share a perspective with the omniscient and benevolent state to whom none are to be lost from view. Greenwood's text, originally generated from within the crisis conjuncture of the early 1930s, is here revived by and for a very different moment, prefiguring and playing its small part in bringing about the social democratic post-war historic bloc that would organise life in Britain for a quarter of a century to come.

Ben Harker

Acknowledgements

I am grateful to Ian Johnston, archivist at the University of Salford library, for his generous assistance with my research in the Walter Greenwood Archive. Thanks also to staff at the Manchester Central Library for access to the Theatre Collection.

Notes

1. Andy Croft, *Red Letter Days: British Fiction of the 1930s* (London: Lawrence and Wishart, 1990), p. 12. Harold Heslop's novel *Last Cage Down* (1935) was republished by Lawrence and Wishart in 1988; Walter Brierley's *Means Test Man* (1939) was republished by Spokesman in 1983; Lewis Jones's novels *Cwmardy* (1937) and *We Live* (1939) were republished by Lawrence and Wishart in 1978.
2. Raymond Williams, *Marxism and Literature* (Oxford: Oxford University Press, 1977), p. 117.
3. Stephen Constantine, '*Love on the Dole* and its reception in the 1930s', *Literature and History* 8.2 (1982), pp. 232–47.
4. The novel drew praise from publications as diverse as *The Spectator* and the *Socialist Review* and was endorsed by Winifred Holtby, Edith Sitwell and Harold Laski. Details of the novel's reception are given in Constantine (1982), p. 234, p. 243 and Matthew Gaughan, 'Palatable socialism or "the real thing"?: Walter Greenwood's *Love on the Dole*', *Literature and History* 17.2 (2008), pp. 47–61.
5. For the novel's silence around the middle-class, see Constantine (1982), p. 237. For a critical account from the left, see Carole Snee, 'Working Class Literature or Proletarian Writing', in Jon Clark, Margot Heinemann, David Margolies and Carole Snee, eds, *Culture and Crisis in Britain in the Thirties* (London: Lawrence and Wishart, 1979), pp. 165–93. Snee argues that Greenwood's ideological line is that of a 'liberal reformer' (p. 171) and that his text is 'a curiously unpolitical novel, with little reference to the political events which had contributed so directly to the misfortunes of those who inhabit Hanky Park' (p. 172). She makes the point that Greenwood omits to mention the General Strike (p. 172) and other political events in 'years of enormous importance to the labour movement' (p. 172). More recently, Stephen Ross has argued that the novel's hierarchy of linguistic registers has the effect of 'implicating [Greenwood] in a bourgeois aesthetic ideology that subverts the novel's ostensibly progressive aims'. Stephen Ross, 'Authenticity Betrayed: the "idiotic folk" of *Love on the Dole*', *Cultural Critique* 56 (Winter 2004), pp. 189–209, p. 192. Chris Hopkins takes a similar position in his *English Fiction in the 1930s: Language, Genre, History* (London: Continuum, 2006), pp. 43–51.
6. Raymond Williams, *Marxism and Literature*, p. 114.
7. Walter Greenwood, *Love on the Dole* (1933; Harmondsworth: Penguin, 1969). The text addresses the National Government and the election of 1931 on pages 164, 179 and 186.
8. Greenwood, *There Was a Time* (London: Jonathan Cape, 1967), pp. 246–9.
9. Greenwood, *Love on the Dole* (London: Jonathan Cape, 1933). The epigraphs were cut from the second edition, restored for the 1969 Penguin reprint, and removed once more from the recent Vintage edition of 1993.
10. Gary Day, for example, argues that Meath's death can be read as 'a sign that the working-class intellectual no longer has a part to play in working-class culture' (Gary Day, *Class* [London: Routledge, 2001], p. 175).

11 Robert Tressell, *The Ragged Trousered Philanthropists* (1914; London: Grafton, 1988).
12 Walter Benjamin, 'The author as producer' (1934) in *Understanding Brecht*, trans. Anna Bostock (London: Verso, 1998), p. 100.
13 Greenwood, *Love on the Dole* (1969), pp. 180–84.
14 Williams, *Marxism and Literature*, p. 114.
15 Georg Lukács, *History and Class Consciousness*, trans. Rodney Livingstone (London: Merlin, 1971), pp. 171–2.
16 For the activities of the Manchester and Salford branches of the WTM in this period, see Ben Harker, *Class Act: The Cultural and Political Life of Ewan MacColl* (London and Ann Arbor: Pluto, 2007), pp. 23–9.
17 The Gow quotation is cited in Ray Speakman's introduction to Ronald Gow and Walter Greenwood, *Love on the Dole* (Oxford: Heinemann, 1986), p. 10. Additional information about Gow's career is from Lawrence Fitch's obituary of Gow, *The Guardian*, 10 May 1993.
18 The original production was reviewed by ASW, 'Love on the Dole: First Night at Repertory Theatre', *Manchester Guardian*, 27 February 1934, R.J. Finnemore, 'Triumph of Love on the Dole', *Daily Dispatch*, 27 February 1934 and Alan Bendle, 'Darker Salford on the Stage: Repertory's Love on the Dole a Hit', *Manchester Evening News*, 27 February 1934.
19 *Daily Express*, 31 January 1935.
20 Hannen Swaffer, 'Tragedy Behind the Play', *Daily Herald*, 1 February 1935.
21 Constantine (1982), p. 233. Constantine explains that the production was raised in parliament by National Liberal cabinet minister Sir Herbert Samuel on 4 March 1935 (p. 234).
22 George Orwell, *The Road to Wigan Pier* (1937; London: Penguin, 2001), pp. 79–80.
23 Ronald Gow and Walter Greenwood, *Love on the Dole: A Play in Three Acts* (London: Jonathan Cape, 1935); Ronald Gow and Walter Greenwood, *Love on the Dole* (1936; London: Samuel French, 1938).
24 The season included Richard Hughes' *Danger*, Harrison Owen's *Doctor Pygmalion* and Campbell Dixon and Dermot Morrah's *Caesar's Friend*. The original programme is archived in the Manchester Central Library Theatre Collection, box TH 792 094273/MA 37. For the mid-1930s programming at the Manchester Repertory Theatre see Harker, *Class Act*, pp. 40–45.
25 Gow and Greenwood, *Love on the Dole* (1935).
26 Greenwood, *Love on the Dole* (1969), p. 86; pp. 180–84.
27 Gow and Greenwood, *Love on the Dole* (1936), p. 9.
28 Benjamin, 'The Author as Producer' (1934), p. 100; Greenwood, *Love on the Dole* (1933), p. 208.
29 Raymond Williams, 'Theatre as a Political Forum' (1988) reprinted in *Politics of Modernism: Against the New Conformists* (London: Verso, 1989), p. 85.
30 Williams, 'Theatre as a Political Forum', p. 85.
31 Meath explains the apprenticeship system to Harry Hardcastle (p. 47); he teaches at the street meeting (p. 86); his first date with Sally is on a Labour Party ramble (pp. 96–7); Mrs Bull recalls his election time activities (p. 164), as does Harry Hardcastle (p. 178); Meath teaches at Marlowe's (pp. 180–81) and is sacked for chalking his lesson on the company wall (p. 186); he gives a speech during the Means Test demonstration calling for 'working-class organization' (p. 199). All page references to Greenwood, *Love on the Dole* (1969).
32 Gow and Greenwood, *Love on the Dole* (1935), p. 20.
33 Gow and Greenwood, *Love on the Dole* (1935), pp. 18–19.
34 Greenwood, *Love on the Dole* (1969), p. 86.
35 Gow and Greenwood, *Love on the Dole* (1935), p. 18.
36 Gow and Greenwood, *Love on the Dole* (1935), p. 81.

37 Greenwood, *Love on the Dole* (1969), p. 135.
38 Narkey hopes for trouble on the demonstration (p. 198) and though not named as Meath's assailant, is prominent in the fray, 'recklessly indiscriminate' (p. 205) with his truncheon (Greenwood, *Love on the Dole* [1969]).
39 Gow and Greenwood, *Love on the Dole* (1935), p. 110.
40 In the novel, Meath is sacked from Marlowe's after chalking political lessons on the wall (1969; p. 186); in both stage adaptations it is the love plot that triggers his redundancy in that Grundy exercises his influence to disadvantage his rival for Sally's affections. Meath, however, is unable to see this; blinded by his tendency to see the world in political terms, he attributes his redundancy to contracting capitalism (Gow and Greenwood, *Love on the Dole* [1935], p. 79).
41 Gow and Greenwood, *Love on the Dole* (1935), pp. 54–5.
42 Gow and Greenwood, *Love on the Dole* (1935), p. 99.
43 Gow and Greenwood, *Love on the Dole* (1935), p. 106.
44 The foundational text of the Popular Front was Dimitrov's speech to the Seventh Congress of the Communist International, published in Britain in 1935. 'Before the establishment of a fascist dictatorship', he stated, 'bourgeois governments usually pass through a number of preliminary stages and institute a number of reactionary measures, which directly facilitate the accession of power to fascism. Whoever does not fight the reactionary measures of the bourgeoisie and the growth of fascism at these preparatory stages, *is not in a position to prevent the victory of fascism, but, on the contrary, facilitates that victory*' [italics in original]. The quotation is from *The Working Class against Fascism: Dimitrov's Speech to the Seventh Congress of the Communist International* (London: Martin Lawrence, 1935), p. 8. A similar line of analysis can be found in popular front publications such as Roger Brady, *The Spirit and Structure of German Fascism* (London: Gollancz, 1937); G.D.H. and M.I. Cole warned against the pro-fascist bias of the police in their *The Condition of Britain* (London: Gollancz, 1937), pp. 434–6.
45 Gow later recalled that the new scene was written to provide parts for two understudies; 'it covered the commotion', he remembers, 'while the audience returned from the bar.' Cited in Ray Speakman's notes to Ronald Gow and Walter Greenwood, *Love on the Dole* (Oxford: Heinemann, 1986), p. 112. Gow agreed to have a lightly edited version of the original scene restored for this 1980s reprint.
46 Gow and Greenwood, *Love on the Dole* (1935), p. 99; Gow and Greenwood, *Love on the Dole* (1936), p. 55.
47 Gow and Greenwood, *Love on the Dole* (1935), p. 102; Gow and Greenwood, *Love on the Dole* (1936), p. 57.
48 See Piers Brendon, *The Dark Valley: A Panorama of the 1930s* (London: Jonathan Cape, 2000), pp. 169–73.
49 Manchester's most radical theatre critic, R.J. Finnemore, cited the play's extended run as evidence of popular demand, poorly served by commercial theatre, for 'plays dealing with topics which commercially are regarded as almost taboo' (R.J. Finnemore, 'Is there a crisis in theatre?', *Daily Dispatch*, 17 May 1935).
50 The first two quotations are from Hannan Swaffer's 'Shakespeare on the Dole: England's Stricken Cities Inspire a Great Play', and *The People*, undated cutting in the Walter Greenwood archive at the University of Salford, file 3/5/1; the third is from Derek Verschoyle, 'The Theatre', *The Spectator*, 8 February 1935.
51 George Orwell, *The Road to Wigan Pier* (1937; London: Penguin, 2001), p. 101.
52 *Daily Mirror*, 31 January 1935.
53 James Agate, 'The Dramatic World: A Lancashire Problem', *The Sunday Times*, 3 February 1935.

54 A.E. Wilson, 'Poverty and Realism: London Takes to "Dole" Play', *The Star*, 31 January 1935; 'My companion, a young and pretty girl', wrote the unsigned *Star* reviewer in a separate article, 'was actually so impressed that she has gone straight off this morning to offer her services to the Personal Service League, which is devoted to doing what can be done to relieve just those conditions which this play so vividly depicts'. Unsigned review, undated cutting from *The Star,* Walter Greenwood Archive 3/1; J.T. Grein, 'Criticism in Cameo', *The Sketch*, 13 February 1935.

55 The first quotation is from Hannan Swaffer, 'Tragedy Behind the Play', *Daily Herald*, 1 February 1935, the second from Hannan Swaffer's 'Shakespeare on the Dole: England's Stricken Cities Inspire a Great Play', *The People*, undated cutting in the Walter Greenwood archive 3/5/1. Greenwood's political activities, widely reported in the press, are highlighted in all three articles.

56 Wilson, *The Star*, 31 January 1935; HFE, untitled review, *Punch*, 13 February 1935.

57 Hannan Swaffer, 'Tragedy Behind the Play', *Daily Herald*, 1 February 1935.

58 Walter Benjamin, 'What is epic theatre?' [First version] (1939) in *Understanding Brecht*, trans. Anna Bostock (London: Verso, 1998), p. 4.

59 Constantine (1982), p. 233. The play was presented at the Shubert Theater, New York, in February 1936, and at the Comédie des Champs-Élysées, Paris, in March 1937.

60 For the class dynamics of 1930s cinema, see Peter Miles and Malcolm Smith, *Cinema, Literature and Society* (London and New York: Croom Helm, 1987), pp. 26–8.

61 For Formby see Miles and Smith, *Cinema*, p. 27 and Keith Williams, *British Writers and the Media, 1930–45* (London: Macmillan, 1996), p. 168.

62 Extracts from the report are quoted in Jeffrey Richards, *The Age of the Dream Palace: Cinema and Society 1930–39* (London and New York: Routledge, 1984), p. 119.

63 Richards, *Dream Palace*, p. 119. The film is also discussed by Tony Williams in *Structures of Desire: British Cinema, 1933–1955* (New York: State University of New York Press, 2000), pp. 73–7.

64 Stuart Hall, 'The Great Moving Right Show', *Marxism Today* (January 1979), pp. 14–20 (p. 15).

65 Harold Nicolson, diary entry 3 July 1940, cited in Williams, *British Writers*, p. 186.

66 Baxter in *Kinematograph Weekly*, 14 January 1943, p. 1030. Cited in Robert Murphy, *Realism and Tinsel: Cinema and Society in Britain 1939–49* (London: Routledge, 1989), p. 25.

67 Miles and Smith, *Cinema*, p. 245.

68 John Baxter, dir., *Love on the Dole* (1941).

69 *Sunday Pictorial*, 1 June 1941. Cited in Richards, *Dream Palace*, pp. 120–21.

70 Williams, *British Writers*, p. 218.

'Ephemeral work': Louis MacNeice and the Moment of 'Pure Radio'

Paul Long

> Content
> To find there was ephemeral work to do,
> Ephemeral work I did.[1]

Introduction

In this paper I want to think about radio as constituting a lost tradition. At the core of this discussion is a particular moment in the UK in which radio generated a range of ideas about its aesthetic possibilities and essence as well as its potential cultural and social role. There are parallels here I think with Raymond Williams's thoughts about film as a lost tradition in progressive cultural politics. For him, this inherently popular and democratic modern medium overcame 'all the cultural barriers which selective education has erected around high literacy'.[2] Williams asked: what had happened to the relationship of that technology and progressive ideas? Was it 'simply to be dumped in that dustbin of history'?[3]

I want to establish a context for thinking about the moment of radio and in order to illuminate some key issues I will explore the early radio practice of Louis MacNeice and his comments on the medium. As I suggest below, MacNeice is an exceptional figure in this lost tradition in that much of his key work has been preserved and is also relatively accessible. His status as a literary figure means that his radio work has attracted attention, although I would argue that critics often treat this work *qua* radio unevenly. Barbara Coulton's extensive professional biography *Louis MacNeice in the BBC* (1980) is more successful in this respect in that she treats radio, like MacNeice did, as something to be *heard* rather than simply read in script form. Coulton outlines MacNeice's broadcast career and deftly relates his literary work to that of his radio productions. Her analysis of the context at the Corporation, some of MacNeice's key productions in relation to his role in the literary scene is an indispensible overview for anyone wishing to understand his achievement and indeed the practices of an era in which radio was the primary broadcast medium.

As Coulton suggests, radio offered a realisation of MacNeice's search for community and communication.[4] I have used this idea as a prompt, concentrating in particular on the origins and development of his ideas and writing on radio in relation to his early practice. I am interested in particular in MacNeice's arguments for the cultural worth and quiddity of the medium, or 'pure radio' as it was known. Through such arguments, he serves as a representative of a wider set of progressive artists and thinkers in the BBC with positive aspirations for a democratic culture that was seeded in the politics of the 1930s.

Retrieving the Sound of Radio as Radio

Michele Hilmes offers a useful argument for thinking about radio in terms of lost and marginalised traditions. She notes that for about forty years radio provided an 'electronic hearth', a 'primary means of negotiating the boundaries between public life and the private home'.[5] Despite the importance of the medium for so long and for so many, she suggests that in terms of any historical and contemporary attention 'this invisible permeation of our lives has gone remarkably unstudied'.[6] One of the reasons for this lack of attention came about with usurpation of radio by TV in the 1950s, at a time when the former had not even begun to attract serious scholarly attention in terms of its aesthetics, cultural and political dimensions as well as its social role.

Although Hilmes has in mind the US context, her ideas are appropriate for an understanding of the UK and for framing the period in which MacNeice worked. His radio career (1941–1963) is enveloped broadly by those years in which the BBC held a monopoly over UK broadcasting (1922–1955), and his particular contribution was to the form and nature of 'features' production that thrived in various guises from the birth of the BBC until the closure of its dedicated Features Department. The Features Department closed in 1964, the same year in which the BBC launched its second TV channel, thus signalling the shift of the Corporation's priorities to the newer medium. 1964 also registered the first sounds of unlicensed commercial offshore radio stations (the misnamed 'pirates') that began to redefine definitions of popular music and to challenge established ideas about audiences and indeed of radio. If we can identify a broad 'age of radio' in the UK here then, its conclusion was marked in the publication of the BBC planning report *Broadcasting in the Seventies* that suggested to one commentator that 'television was now completely in the saddle […] the word was being demoted'.[7]

The consequences of the demotion of radio with the coming of TV are described by Hilmes in terms of a massive act of public 'forgetting' of the medium, its history and practices. She notes a consequent parallel in the academy too, suggesting that when compared to the manner in which film and TV have been studied, radio has presented a 'theoretical impossibility' for scholars who have largely chosen to ignore its significance and signification. More recently however, this amnesia and the lack of attention afforded radio has begun to be addressed in scholarly work, and 'The "missing decades" of the '30s and '40s, in particular, have captured the imaginations of cultural historians'.[8]

The focus on this period offers potential challenges given the fact that the vast majority of the prodigious output of early radio is unrecoverable in its live broadcast form. We can note therefore that one of the explanations for any neglect is contingent on the technology and practices of the formative years of radio production that made its output ephemeral. For a long time, it was not deemed necessary, desirable or indeed possible, at least with any fidelity, to record radio programmes for repeat broadcast or for posterity.[9]

In his memoirs, the BBC writer and producer D.G. Bridson noted the individual consequences of the ephemeral aspect of radio production. Over his thirty-five years at the BBC as writer or producer, his name was associated with around eight hundred productions, yet regretfully 'there was certainly little tangible to show at the end of it [...] few of my scripts had been published, and not many of my shows survived even in recorded form. For the rest, they were blowing in the wind indeed'.[10] In MacNeice's case we are luckier to have more substantial material. Produced over twenty years, his *oeuvre* numbers original creations, adaptations and translations including versions of Goethe's *Faust* (*tx* 30 October–21 November 1949) and classical fictions such as Apuleius' *The Golden Ass* (*tx* 3 November 1944). MacNeice's colleague R.D. ('Reggie') Smith counted over one hundred and fifty scripts of MacNeice's in the BBC Play Library,[11] although, as Coulton has discovered, the archive is by no means complete.[12] Nonetheless, that radio has its own canon and has been subject to the kind of 'selective tradition' identified by Raymond Williams seems apparent.

MacNeice and Cultural Politics in the 1930s

MacNeice's reputation as a poet was cemented in the 1930s and it is useful to consider his place in this context and contemporary cultural debates in tracing his move to the BBC. His status as a literary star is indicated in a comment from Geoffrey Grigson who wrote of him that 'I believe that there is no other poet now in England who is such a good *writer*'.[13] MacNeice contributed verse, criticism and comment to John Lehmann's *New Writing*, Grigson's *New Verse*, the *Listener*, amongst others, as well as producing prose works and dramatic work for the innovative Group Theatre.

'Ephemeral work': Louis MacNeice and the Moment of 'Pure Radio'

Looking back at this period in 1941, George Orwell described the fractious cultural politics of the 1930s and the way in which literature was swamped with 'propaganda'. He suggested that 'the characteristic writers of the time, people like Auden and Spender and MacNeice, have been didactic, political writers, aesthetically conscious, of course, but more interested in subject-matter than in technique'.[14] In fact, amidst the political polarities of this milieu, MacNeice's position was not so simple to label. Peter McDonald relates how the dust jacket of MacNeice's *Poems* (1935) described the author as 'intensely serious without political enthusiasm', as if to distance his work from contemporary questions of commitment.[15] Yet MacNeice was not unengaged with contemporary cultural issues nor quiet about questions of social justice and politics, even if he felt it difficult to commit to any dogmatic position, especially any that made *a priori* claims on his creative work. Edna Longley quotes a passage in *I Crossed the Minch* (1938) and a dialogue between MacNeice and his imaginary guardian angel that gives a broad sense of his political sensibility. For the poet, the question of his personal politics was inconsequential, but when pushed he revealed that: 'My sympathies are Left. On paper and in the soul. But not in my heart or my guts. On paper – yes.'[16]

Orwell's remarks indicate the contemporary importance of questions concerning the political in art as well as the politics of access to and social use of culture. Something of this is captured in a polemic launched by Grigson against what he labelled wryly as the 'arts end' of the *New Statesman*. He complained of 'hierophants' at odds with the socialist ethos of the 'other end' of the journal, that 'a band of skinless and sensitive manikins worship and protect *culture* [original emphasis], which lies hidden, like the bones of a dead saint, in a Louis Quinze commode, behind a silk curtain'.[17] What was at stake for the privileged was best summarised in MacNeice's own *Autumn Journal* (1939) which, as Samuel Hynes has suggested, is 'the best personal expression of the end-of-the-'thirties mood'.[18] Conscious of his privileged position and role within this system of inequality, MacNeice wrote of how his habitual thinking exposed his own sympathies that:

To preserve the values dear to the élite
The élite must remain a few. It is hard to imagine
A world where the many would have their chance without
A fall in the standard of intellectual living
And nothing left that the highbrow cared about.[19]

Here we can turn to consider the place of the BBC in contemporary debates over culture. The BBC's first Director General, Sir John Reith, had lofty ambitions for broadcasting; his idea of what was valuable derived from a Presbyterian desire for moral soundness. As Roger Sales observes:

> He wanted it to take the high cultural road and educate popular taste rather than merely pander to the lowest common denominator. There was thus a heavy stress on the best that had been thought, written, known and heard. Reith's book of prophecies, *Broadcasting Over Britain* (1924), was a mixture of the theocratic ramblings of a Carlyle with the cultural poise of an Arnold.[20]

The resultant character of the BBC accounts for the ambivalent place it held in British life from its inception. Thinking of the role of broadcasting and other media in contemporary social consciousness, Charles Madge offered a measured assessment of the Corporation when he suggested that 'it would be undialectic to suppose that the B.B.C. is unmixed, either as curse or blessing'.[21] Certainly, many intellectuals shared Reith's objectives and signed up to this project, notably T.S. Eliot, who hoped to use this mass medium in a way that counteracted its baser impulses.[22] However, such paternalism meant that for progressive producers such as Bridson, at least before he joined the BBC, the institution was firmly bracketed with Parliament, the Monarchy and the Church. As he recalled in his memoir, the BBC 'stood for order and orthodoxy, the *status quo* and all that the *status quo* implied when the economy was dying on its feet'.[23] Certainly, the character of those who dominated the airwaves, the schedules and the agenda seemed to echo the priorities of the establishment. As Madge commented: 'the listeners are legion, but the voices which speak are few.'[24]

For other intellectuals such as Virginia Woolf, Reith's aspirations were diluted in practice. For her, the initials BBC stood for 'betwixt and between' culture, indicating the so-called 'middlebrow' quality of its output, an inevitable aspect of broadcasting. The view was that while Reith had lofty cultural ambitions, the aim to reach out to a mass audience resulted in productions pitched at an average level in order to appeal to the majority of listeners.[25] Woolf advised Stephen Spender that for poets and other writers to work for the BBC was thus to imperil their art amidst its cultural blandness.[26] MacNeice initially shared this disdain, as he later recalled: 'Before I joined the BBC I was, like most of the intelligentsia, prejudiced not only against that institution but against broadcasting in general.'[27]

With experience, MacNeice would change his mind about broadcasting, although some of his thoughts on cultural democracy suggest that the BBC, whatever its faults, was always a logical destination for him. He wrote in *Modern Poetry* (1938) of his preference for poets 'whose worlds are not too esoteric' and who are connected with ordinary life and ordinary people. While disagreeing with the dogmatic prescriptions for politically aligned art of writers such as Edward Upward, he suggested that it was 'probably true' that for production of major literature 'a sympathy is required in the writer with those forces which at the moment make for progress'.[28] Ultimately, MacNeice's progressive cultural politics are best expressed in his rejoinder to those elitist sentiments in *Autumn Journal*. Writing of the need to suppress those negative feelings he had articulated so well, he commented that

> [...] There is no reason for thinking
> That, if you give a chance to people to think or live,
> The arts of life will suffer and become rougher
> And not return more than you could ever give.[29]

And it was at the BBC that the chance to explore the challenge of these sentiments would be worked out.

Inventing Sounds

MacNeice took up the offer of a post in the BBC in 1941. He had been teaching in America when war broke out and, like Auden and Isherwood, had the opportunity to stay there for the duration. He was, however, upset both by the neutrality of America, expressed in the blasé attitudes to the war of some of his students, as well as that of the Irish Republic.[30] R.D. Smith records a letter home from MacNeice from the period which expressed the ethos that lay behind his decision to return to the UK: 'freedom means Getting Into Things, not Getting Out of Them.'[31]

As MacNeice was medically unfit for service, the move to the BBC might have been a sensible one for a poet and classicist eager to do something for the collective effort. The logic of this move and the opportunities presented by the BBC were again anticipated in *Modern Poetry* where he suggested that poets should be encouraged to write dramatic verse, that 'they may find a good medium in radio plays [...] It is very good for the poet that he should employ certain forms which demand collaboration with other craftsmen. A poet should always be "collaborating" with his public'.[32] Equally, MacNeice would have read Herbert Read's 'open letter' to the Director General of the BBC in *New Verse* in which Read opined that 'it is in the power of radio to revive poetry as a spoken art'. In broadcasting, Read wrote, it would be possible to reinvent poetry in a new bardic manner, removing it from the taint of ink and the literary field: 'There must be many experiments, not only in the composition of poems, but also in the speaking of poems [...] We must get rid of the idea that poetry can be read, or announced, or even recited. Poetry must be composed by the voice [...] It must be treated as a new art – an art to be discovered by vast circles of dumb listeners.' This would be a means of saving poets from the solipsistic 'underground life'.[33]

MacNeice was recruited to the Drama and Features Department, which was then under the overall direction of its founder Val Gielgud. Gielgud's deputy was Laurence Gilliam, who oversaw the production of features and liked to recruit creative individuals such as MacNeice, encouraging them to explore the medium and to innovate freely. The wealth of poetic talent in Features was such that in one later article in *Picture Post* the department was labelled 'A Nest of Singing Birds'.[34] The BBC feature was celebrated by its various producers as *the* radio art form. For Gilliam, it was the culmination of the medium, a capturing of its quintessence: 'It is pure radio, a new instrument for the creative writer and producer.'[35] However, the feature was nonetheless a creature of uncertain identity. Although it was not conceived as reportage, for Bridson the feature 'had been developed notably as a medium for creative writing of a new order'.[36] Taking a cue from the film documentaries of the 1930s, the feature tended to deal with aspects of 'actuality' as an opportunity for bringing the poetic and journalistic together.[37] Another commentator suggested that 'features recreate fact [...] in this respect they are a development of talks, but with several distinct advantages of their own; features are more powerful in their effect; they can appeal to emotion as well as to reason [...] through their exploitation of dramatic elements'.[38]

During the war, the Drama and Features Department was tasked with making a 'contribution to the preservation of civilised culture'.[39] Perhaps not always entirely distinguishable from such a role, its purpose was also defined as producing 'implicit or explicit propagandist contributions to national wartime activity'.[40] MacNeice's first work was produced under this rubric and included a series entitled *The Stones Cry Out*, which addressed both concerns creatively, melding the journalistic and the poetic. Ostensibly conceived as documentary, the series explored the stories of a range of iconic buildings under threat from the blitz, around which themes of endurance could be explored and expressed. As it was announced at the start of each episode: 'The people stand firm: but the stones cry out!' The sites portrayed include Westminster Abbey, the House of Commons and Madame Tussauds, allowing an exploration of ideas about what was being fought for (culture, idiosyncracy and individualism, freedom) as well as what was being fought against (barbarism, tyranny, obedience). Based in the lexicographer's house, *Dr Johnson Takes It* (*tx* 5 May 1941) exhibits the kinds of approach MacNeice brought to the programmes he produced from the outset. It employs a strikingly urgent counterpoint of two voices reciting contrasting and competing lexicons. A gentle female voice begins, followed by a grim and foreboding male voice.

> Female voice: A is for Art
> Male voice: A is for Arson
> Female voice: B is for Bookcase
> Male Voice: B is for Bomb
> Female voice: C is for Courage
> Male voice: C is for Corpse
> Female voice: D is for Dictionary
> Male voice: D is for Death
> Female voice: E is for English
> Male voice: E is for Evil
> Female voice: F is for Future
> Male voice: F is for Fire!

This last line is delivered emphatically, punctuated by a musical crescendo emulating the conflagration and force of the Blitz and its threat to the future and all of those positive things listed by the female voice. The male voice, while conveying the sense of threat, may also be heard as that of defiance and stoic resilience.

MacNeice was quickly handed responsibility for a series of prestigious productions. He adapted Sergei Eisenstein's 1938 film *Alexander Nevsky* (*tx* 8 December 1941) for the air, using the score written for it by Prokofiev. This was conceived as a propagandist piece also, commissioned as part of a mission to alter attitudes to Russia, now an ally, which had been invaded in June 1941. *Christopher Columbus* (*tx* 12 October 1942) was written to celebrate the 450th anniversary of the explorer's first voyage of discovery and also served as an expression of support of the new ally, with the US entry into the war after the attack on Pearl Harbor.

Christopher Columbus was a significant broadcast 'event'. It was unusually lengthy and had music from William Walton who had scored the propagandist movies *First of the Few*, *Went the Day Well* (both 1942) and was later to score Laurence Olivier's *Henry V* (1944), and who was given access to the full resources of the BBC's Music Department. There was considerable appreciation at the time for the interplay of the music and MacNeice's 'irregular blank verse'.[41] MacNeice conveyed a sense of one key sequence, which involved Columbus's procession from Seville to Barcelona. This was accompanied throughout by processional music: 'this meant that the running commentaries in verse during these sequences were delivered, over the music, with much the same tempo and punch that characterise a real running commentary delivered over the noise of a crown on a sportsground. Walton's music, I should add, served its purpose admirably; i.e. it was structural.'[42] (Sporting programmes and concerts were some of the few radio forms MacNeice paid attention to before he joined the BBC.)

He Had a Date (*tx* 28 June 1944) was another signal work of this period. It dealt with a difficult subject in an innovative but emotionally sensitive treatment, dramatising the moment of death of a sailor going down with his torpedoed ship. It merged internal monologue, the exchange of voices from moments in this life and snippets of popular music to convey time, feeling and sentiment. A very personal story, it was inspired by the loss of one of MacNeice's closest friends in just such an incident, and is one of a minority of works in the mass media made during wartime to deal with loss in such an explicitly emotive fashion.[43]

Another radio 'event' was *The Dark Tower* (*tx* 21 January 1946). Written immediately after the war, this play is repeatedly singled out as MacNeice's finest radio work, for some the crowning achievement of the age of 'pure radio'. This was a conscious attempt at a modern parable, inspired by Henrik Ibsen's *Peer Gynt*, Franz Kafka's stories and Thomas Mann's *The Magic Mountain*.[44] Taking an immediate cue from Robert Browning's 'Childe Roland to the Dark Tower Came', *The Dark Tower* concerns another Roland whose role in life appeared to be simply to prepare for a preordained and fatal moment of destiny. Embarking upon a quest, Roland travels across a symbolic landscape to the dark tower of the title in order to confront what could be a literal or figurative dragon. The dragon of *The Dark Tower* appears to embody the evil that mankind must perpetually deal with and struggle to overcome. With its tropes of informants, persecution, free will and responsibility, *The Dark Tower* seems most readily to be a reference to fascism and the struggle of the war itself, but it is hard to pin down to any direct parallel. It certainly avoids the didacticism MacNeice was accused of perpetrating in his poems. MacNeice himself commented: 'Do not ask me what Ism it illustrates or what Solution it offers.'[45]

Within its parable form, what is particularly interesting about *The Dark Tower* is the manner in which MacNeice incorporates a motif of self-consciousness into the actions of the characters. This aspect of the play speaks to the authorial act of creation and to how radio itself works. An illustrative scene comes when Roland begins his quest and meets an old alcoholic, 'The Soak', at a port. Invited to a tavern, Roland declines and in response this character announces that 'If you won't come to the tavern, the tavern must come to you'. He calls for music, whereupon the soundtrack orchestra strikes up. Literally orchestrating this musical creation, 'The Soak' announces that:

> Music can build a palace, let alone a pub.
> Come on you masons of the Muses, swing it,
> Fling me up four walls. Now, now, don't drop your tempo;
> Easy with those hods. All right; four walls.
> Now benches – tables – No! No doors or windows.
> What drunk wants daylight? But you've left out the bar.
> Come on – 'Cellos! Percussion! All of you! A bar!
> That's right. Dismiss!
> (*The music ends*).

This motif becomes ever more apparent and complex as 'The Soak' speaks with Roland as if he were also, like the music, 'my projection'. Once 'The Soak' drops off into drunken sleep the hero's doubts about his status and purpose exacerbate. He muses to himself:

> If I were something existing in his mind
> How could I go on now that he's asleep?

To which The Soak replies, muffled, still dreaming:

> Because I'm dreaming you [...]
> You'd never guess, young man, what role I've cast you for –

This last line underlines the motif of self-consciousness in the play, paralleling Roland's personal journey to discover the nature of his purpose and actions and also echoing MacNeice's own commitment to 'get into' things at the outset of war. Roland's progression towards unequivocal and selfless action counters his indulgent solipsism and resulting doubt. He describes himself as 'the black sheep, the unbeliever – Who never did anything of his own free will –', and is forced to act and overcome his fear of committing to the eternal struggle, inviting the dragon inhabiting the dark tower to 'Come out and do your worst'. Through his act of commitment and its demonstration, Roland serves to 'bequeath free will to others'.

In many ways this play was an arch exercise in form, based on MacNeice's conclusion that 'pure "realism" is in our time played out'.[46] Philip Hope Wallace, writing in the *Listener*, called *The Dark Tower* 'An uncouth modern edifice', cautioning that many great writers had taken on the quest theme only to bore their audiences. For him, the play was difficult to visualise although he acknowledged that visualisation was perhaps not MacNeice's intention. He concluded with more enthusiasm that 'we were conscious of a real poet's sensibility, of a wide power of matching new-minted phrase and stale jargon to make a language which should touch heart and mind and ear freshly'.[47]

Theorising Sound

These early radio works suggest how MacNeice accommodated the technical demands of the medium and how he engaged positively with and tested its aesthetic possibilities. His BBC colleague William Empson testified to MacNeice's immediate impact as a producer during the war, recalling that 'You could show him the rough material [...] and he knew at once what you could put over, what would do. Even with quite a complicated script, one runthrough would be quite enough [...] he was always unruffled and very much the captain of his ship'.[48] MacNeice's works speak of high aspirations for the medium, according with some aspects of the Reithian ideal for broadcasting. These were consciously high cultural exercises which enlisted the aid of contemporary names in the arts: composers William Walton on *Christopher Columbus*, Benjamin Britten on *The Dark Tower* and renowned actors of the day such as Robert Donat and Laurence Olivier, all contributed to making such works radio 'events'.

MacNeice was also continuing the work of a minority in the BBC who had sought to explore the nature of radio *qua* radio. Such practice was distinct from an approach which treated radio as a simple acoustic transmitter, a transparent medium for events and ideas, or existing plays, songs or poems, whose meanings and forms were determined elsewhere. Attending to the materiality of radio meant exploring what it could achieve as a distinctive modern cultural form in relation to a mass audience. Thus, by the 1930s, radio drama technique was well-developed in terms of devices such as 'internal monologue, the swift, sharpcut cinema reel of a life flashing through the mind of a dying person, sound effects verbally places and primed, music as function not decoration', all of which MacNeice employed to great effect.[49] Producers like Val Gielgud, L. du Garde Peach, Tyrone Guthrie and Lance Sieveking developed these techniques as they sought to explore the essential aesthetic properties of the medium in their dramatic work.[50] Sean Street cites plays such as *Comedy of Danger* and *The White Chateau* (both 1925), which demonstrated how 'a new style and a new philosophy was not only possible, but necessary'.[51] As Street reports, Sieveking's *Kaleidoscope 1* (1929) employed over a hundred cast members and several studios, lauded by the *Radio Times* as 'a play too purely radio to be printed for reading'.[52]

MacNeice's scripts for *Christopher Columbus* (1944) and *The Dark Tower* (1947) were published soon after broadcast and, alongside other pronouncements, advertised his commitment to the medium in spite of the continuing disapproval of it amongst sections of the intelligentsia.[53] Indicative of this attitude was one trenchant reviewer who took *The Dark Tower* as evidence that radio would affect MacNeice's powers negatively, 'depreciating for the poet the value of individual words'.[54] Taking on such arguments, MacNeice prefaced both published plays with meditations on the nature and value of radio, indicating the degree to which he had become an articulate champion for its form and the wider cultural status he felt it exhibited and could continue to achieve, particularly in its relationship with a mass audience.

In his introduction to *Christopher Columbus*, MacNeice expressed his aspiration to 'interest some members of the more literary public in a popular art-form which still is an art-form'.[55] He noted that radio was afforded little serious critical attention, which was paradoxical when broadcasts gained vast audiences in comparison to stage, novels or poetry. For him, the problem lay not in the quality of much of radio but in the fact that the ephemeral nature of broadcasting meant that there was no chance for another review of its output at leisure. Furthermore, those responsible for the few available critical assessments of radio had yet to appreciate both aims and limitations of the medium. Thus, those who bought books (i.e. those inclined to read his script because it had on it the name of a poet) were still 'very ignorant' of radio; not that they necessarily ever listened.[56]

With such readers in mind then, MacNeice warned that when radio plays and features were confined to the page they lost far more than material written for the theatre. He highlighted the obviousness of the essential qualities of radio, that it was sound 'and sound alone', which defined the medium. This meant that while radio was built on good scripts, it did not necessarily result in good writing. Writing for radio necessarily eschewed many of the subtleties and superfluities of the page as writers had to imagine 'words-as-they-are-spoken – and words-as-they-are-heard'.[57] While sound presented limitations such as a need for exposition, MacNeice wrote of the compensations when compared to theatre. For instance: 'you can take many more liberties with time and place; you are free of the dead hand of the Three Act tradition. You can jump from India to the Arctic and from 1066 to 1943.'[58] The economy of radio was such that it allowed writers and producers to create settings that theatre, and possibly even film, could not recreate or reach. It achieved something more challenging than such forms because for him, 'sound alone is for most people more potent, more pregnant, more subtle, than pictures alone'.[59] Radio, like print, had its own 'proper autonomy', and while the obvious strength of the medium lay in a realism produced through immediacy and topicality, greater potential lay in reaching beyond life, in simplifying and stylising it, 'competing with the Soviet art-cinema rather than with Hollywood or the standardised news-reel'.[60]

In 1954 MacNeice won the *Prix d'Italia* for *Prisoner's Progress* (*tx* 27 April 1954), an international award marking his status as a radio artist. By this time, he was fully at home in the medium and a sense of his creative approach to it is pithily articulated in his poem of the same year, *Autumn Sequel* (itself broadcast as a MacNeice production in six parts from June 1954). While Coulton suggests that this allegorical narrative poem exhibits a 'lack of enthusiasm, an aspect of the sterility which seems to have come on him' in this period, it expresses a lyrical idea of 'pure radio' and what was involved in its making.[61] Here, MacNeice wrote of his job that it involved:

> Not matching pictures but inventing sound,
> Precalculating microphone and knob
>
> In homage to the human voice. To found
> A castle in the air requires a mint
> Of golden intonations and a mound
>
> Of typescript in the trays.[62]

This passage encapsulates MacNeice's sense of the materiality of the medium, of how technology and technique transform the written word and construct a performance in sound, thus giving form to radio as a distinctive art. The value of this creative endeavour is conveyed in the evocation of the Gospel of John, supporting and supported by the authority of the Logos:

> [...] What was in print
> Must take on breath and what was thought be said
> In the end there was the Word.[63]

In his arguments for the value of radio, MacNeice was also mindful of the ways in which dismissals of the medium translated to attitudes towards its audiences. For him, those who considered radio to involve a flattening of standards to a common denominator based their thinking on a dubious conflation of the popular with the vulgar, which 'rests on a misconception of our old friend, the Man-in-the-Street'.[64] Acknowledging that any radio audience included people with a range of intellects and abilities who would cope to varying degrees with the demands of different ideas and issues, MacNeice suggested that radio drama could reach out to audiences as individuals with independent and equivalent sensibilities: 'I refuse to believe that men and women in the street are as insensitive or as emotionally atrophied as is sometimes assumed by the intelligentsia.'[65]

Nonetheless, MacNeice revealed a common intellectual prejudice in arguing that 'ordinary people', while not plagued by innate bad taste, were rather susceptible to a conditioning to like 'what is vulgar and emotionally false'.[66] However, if radio were treated seriously, its virtue was that it could overcome this conditioning rather than reinforce it. Its challenge as a mass medium in communicating with an audience was to rise above the clamour of the modern world.[67] Echoing Herbert Read's hope for how poetry could be reinvigorated by broadcasting, MacNeice suggested that radio had a bardic function similar to those who originally declaimed the tales of Homer or the Icelandic sagas.

For MacNeice to see in radio the potential for modernising a folk tradition, in tandem with his faith in reaching the audience, was at odds with those contemporaries who expressed pessimism in their view that all mass media were inevitably debased and debasing. Many intellectuals, most famously the Leavises and those of the Frankfurt School, saw in mass media products a bland and formulaic character designed to satisfy the anonymous millions, those embodied in that construction of 'The Man-in-the-Street', which so bothered MacNeice. In particular, the nature of culture as *industry*, in Adorno and Horkheimer's famous formulation – in film, press, popular music, literature and radio – militated against the expression of the original individual spirit. Administrative thinking and bureaucratic organisation were inimical to authentic art.

MacNeice takes on such ideas in *Autumn Sequel*. As an artist his job is to create 'castles in the air', but such a romantic notion is grounded by the banal realities of a carpeted office space, the sound of tapping of typewriters and secretarial shorthand. All of these symbolise the organised and reductive mechanisation of the creative process itself by the institutional apparatus of the BBC, which must also be reckoned with:

> [...] and carapaced
> Administrators crouch on constant guard
> To save it for good business and good taste.[68]

Certainly, the impositions and limits of this system were acknowledged by MacNeice who, no lover of institutions himself, noted that it was not 'a good channel for souls in flux, for the kind of inspiration that sings and does not count the cost'.[69] However, it was an obvious fact that 'an organisation working on such a scale cannot depend entirely on spontaneity and must therefore partly rely upon such writers as are prepared to practise radio-writing as a *craft*'.[70] While this situation might be repugnant to some as incompatible with true art, for him, it reproduced the traditional relationship of patron, professional artist and audience. Radio continued this respectable dynamic and relied upon something that self-absorbed literati often neglected, the need to *communicate*. The pleasure of radio work for MacNeice was in a 'thing-being-performed and shared'. In this aspect he found rewards that were lacking in his literary endeavour:

> we have a means by which written lines can emulate the impact of a stage or of a painting and give the writer that excitement of a sensuous experience simultaneously shared with many which is one of the joys of life.[71]

In radio too there was a pleasant aspect to working collectively that was unavailable in the world of poetry, where technique was wedded to the intimately personal voice. While a popular assumption had it that creative workers at the BBC resembled civil servants, he rejected this image, comparing his department to 'almost any contemporary salon of literati'.[72] He wrote of his colleagues that in comparison with many other intellectuals, they were 'quicker-witted, more versatile, less egocentric, less conventional, more humane'.[73]

In these thoughts on the value of radio, MacNeice found an articulation and extension of the progressive ideas in his own musings in *Modern Poetry*, as well as in wider arguments from the 1930s on the need for cultural work that was grounded in the everyday world and in touch with the audience.[74] *Autumn Sequel*, affirms the value of such work as properly creative and worthy of the endeavour of the author himself or of any of his peers:

> If poets must live [...]
> they might find this mess
>
> No more a mess than wasting wits and ink
> On scratching each other's backs or possibly eyes
> Out or half out.[75]

MacNeice and the 'End' of Radio

Appositely, poetically even, MacNeice's end came in 1963, the year before the closure of the Features Department (it had been devolved from Drama at the end of the war) to which he gave and owed so much. His death by pneumonia came as a result of his fieldwork on his final production *Persons From Porlock* (tx 30 August 1963). MacNeice's biographer, Jon Stallworthy, relates a well-worn and instructive tale about those last days.[76] A note from BBC administrators pointed out that he had not made a programme in several months. Asked what he was doing, he responded that he had been 'thinking'. A function of this story is to convey something about the changes in the nature of the BBC in that period and the changing nature of how public service broadcasting and its possibilities were conceived at the end of an era of 'pure radio'.

Of the Features Department, Lewis Foreman has said that it 'was active with ambitious radio plays and features with music and they quickly accumulated a considerable repertoire so powerful in its style and assumptions that it was not many years before it stimulated a backlash [as] many felt it to be an outmoded and stilted genre'.[77] Radio, and the particular ambitions and innovations of the small but committed group in Features, were usurped by the shift to television, which brought a modernity invested in the visual. In the UK, with the advent of ITV in 1955, this newer version of modernity was intimately bound to a growing consumer society, in which modes of the popular and relations between audiences and creative workers and institutions were undergoing transformation.

In pondering the ephemeral nature of radio in his memoirs, D.G. Bridson asked how many millions had listened to what he had to say, wondering how many of them recalled any of it, how many were influenced by his desire to impact upon the world through his programmes. Whatever doubts he had, he considered that he had tried and, nonetheless, the kind of radio he and his colleagues had made had given a lead in making the world a better place and in contributing to a more just society. In considering MacNeice's place in this context there are questions to consider about the degree to which his work was successful with those with whom he sought to communicate. Perhaps the security of the celebration and preservation of his work should lead us to consider what else from the moment of 'pure radio' and its practices we might retrieve from the 'dustbin of history', to listen again for

> […] this commons of the air
> Which closes such great gaps, yet also fails
> To open such great vistas.[78]

Acknowledgements

Thanks are due to those who aided in the development of this article. Members of The Radio Studies Network proved to be generous in locating available radio work by MacNeice. Particular thanks to Chris Priestman, Amanda Wrigley, Sean Street, David Hendy, Martin Dibbs, Virginia Madsen and Tim Wall. My appreciation extends also to staff of the British Library Sound Archives, Gerry Harrison and finally to Jenny Doctor for encouragement.

Notes

1. Louis MacNeice, *Autumn Sequel* (London: Faber and Faber, 1954), p. 31.
2. Raymond Williams, 'Cinema and Socialism', in *Politics of Modernism: Against the New Conformists* (London: Verso, 1989), p. 107.
3. Williams, p. 107.
4. Barbara Coulton, *Louis MacNeice in the BBC* (London: Faber and Faber, 1980), p. 193. See also the accounts of MacNeice's BBC colleagues: Dallas Bower, 'MacNeice: Sound and Vision' and R.D. Smith, 'Castle on the Air', both in Terence Brown and Alec Reid, eds, *Time Was Away: The World of Louis MacNeice* (Dublin: Dolmen Press, 1974), pp. 97–102, pp. 87–96 and Christopher Holme, 'The Radio Drama of Louis MacNeice', in John Drakakis, ed., *British Radio Drama* (Cambridge and London: Cambridge University Press, 1981), pp. 37–71. A recent work of value is Amanda Wrigley, 'Louis MacNeice's Radio Classics: "all so unimaginably different?"', in Dunstan Lowe and Kim Shahabudin, eds, *Classics For All: Reworking Antiquity in Mass Culture* (Newcastle: Cambridge Scholars Publishing, 2007), pp. 39–61. For background and archival materials for this article I have also drawn on the 1977 BBC TV documentary *Pure Radio* by Philip Donnellan (for further information, see www.philipdonnellan.com).
5. Michelle Hilmes, 'Rethinking Radio', in Michele Hilmes and Jason Loviglio, eds, *Radio Reader: Essays in the Cultural History of Radio* (London and New York: Routledge, 2002), p. 1.
6. Hilmes, p. 2.
7. BBC, *Broadcasting in the Seventies* (London: British Broadcasting Corporation, 1969); George Ewart Evans, *Spoken History* (London: Faber and Faber, 1987), p. 144.
8. Hilmes, p. 2. See also Kate Lacey, 'Ten Years of Radio Studies: The Very Idea', *The Radio Journal – International Studies in Broadcast and Audio Media* 6.1 (2008), pp. 21–32.
9. Similar problems are faced in the retrieval of early television drama, see: Jason Jacobs, *The Intimate Screen: Early British TV Drama* (Oxford: Oxford University Press, 2000).
10. D.G. Bridson, *Prospero and Ariel: The Rise and Fall of Radio, a Personal Recollection* (London: Victor Gollancz, 1971), pp. 333–4.
11. R.D. Smith, 'Radio Scripts 1941–1963', in Terence Brown and Alec Reid, eds, *Time Was Away: The World of Louis MacNeice* (Dublin: Dolmen Press, 1974), pp. 141–8.
12. E.g. Coulton, p. 111.
13. 'G.E.G', 'New Poems by MacNeice and Prokosh', in *New Verse* 30 (Summer 1938), p. 19. Emphasis in original.
14. See: Peter Davison, ed., *The Complete Works of George Orwell: Vol. 12, A Patriot After All – 1940–1941* (London: Secker and Warburg, 1998), p. 484.
15. Quoted in Peter McDonald, *Louis MacNeice: The Poet in His Contexts* (Oxford: Clarendon Press, 1991), p. 12. More recently Richard Danson Brown has taken issue with how MacNeice's place in the period is regularly narrated. See: *Louis MacNeice and the Poetry of the 1930s* (Hornson: Northcote House, 2009).
16. Quoted in Edna Longley, *Louis MacNeice: A Study* (London: Faber and Faber, 1998), p. 39. On MacNeice's politics in comparison with statements from some of his contemporaries see also *New Verse* 11 (October 1934).
17. 'G.E.G', 'Remarks', in *New Verse* 29 (March 1938), p. 13.
18. Samuel Hynes quoted in Edna Longley, *Poetry in the Wars* (London: Bloodaxe, 1986), p. 78.

19. Louis MacNeice, *Autumn Journal* (1939; London: Faber and Faber, 1998), p. 9
20. Roger Sales, 'An Introduction to Broadcasting History', in David Punter, ed., *Introduction to Contemporary Cultural Studies* (London: Longman, 1986), p. 48.
21. Charles Madge, 'Press, Radio, and Social Consciousness', in C. Day Lewis, ed., *The Mind in Chains: Socialism and the Cultural Revolution* (London: Frederick Muller, 1937), p. 158.
22. See Todd Avery, *Radio Modernism: Literature, Ethics, and the BBC, 1922–1938* (Aldershot: Ashgate, 2006), p. 115 and Michael Coyle, 'T.S. Eliot on the Air: "Culture" and the Challenges of Mass Communication', in Jewel Spears Brooker, ed., *T.S. Eliot and Our Turning World* (New York: St Martin's Press, 2001), pp. 141–54.
23. Bridson, p. 31. For a more detailed account of such attitudes see also D.L. LeMahieu, *A Culture for Democracy: Mass Communication and the Cultivated Mind in Britain Between the Wars* (Oxford: Clarendon Press, 1988).
24. Madge, p. 158.
25. On this point, see Kate Lacey, 'Radio in the Great Depression: Promotional Culture, Public Service, and Propaganda', in Hilmes, p. 27
26. Stephen Spender quoted in Paul Muldoon's radio documentary, *In the Dark Tower: Louis MacNeice at the BBC*, BBC (tx 6 January 2007); on Woolf and the BBC see Jonathan Rose, *The Intellectual Life of the British Working Classes* (New Haven and London: Yale University Press, 2001), p. 436.
27. Louis MacNeice, *The Dark Tower* (1947; London: Faber, 1964), p. 11.
28. Louis MacNeice, *Modern Poetry: A Personal Essay* (2nd edition; 1938; Oxford: Clarendon Press, 1968), p. 204. The specific piece he refers to is Edward Upward, 'A Marxist Interpretation of Literature', in Day Lewis, ed., pp. 39–48.
29. MacNeice, *Autumn Journal*, p. 9.
30. See Richard Weight, *Patriots: National Identity in Britain: 1940–2000* (London: Macmillan, 2000), p. 61.
31. Quoted in Smith, 'Castle on the Air', p. 88.
32. Louis MacNeice, *Modern Poetry*, p. 196.
33. Herbert Read 'An Open Letter: To the New Director of the British Broadcasting Corporation', in *New Verse* 31-2 (Autumn 1938), p. 11.
34. As described by Andrew Lycett, *Dylan Thomas: A New Life* (London: Weidenfeld and Nicolson, 2003), p. 229. On the BBC radio feature see Kate Whitehead, *The Third Programme: A Literary History* (Oxford: Clarendon Press, 1989), pp. 109–34.
35. Quoted in Whitehead, p. 113.
36. Bridson, p. 122.
37. On this link see Donnellan's TV documentary *Pure Radio*. For the aesthetics of documentary see: John Grierson, 'Untitled Lecture on Documentary', in Ian Aitken, ed., *The Documentary Film Movement: An Anthology* (Edinburgh: Edinburgh University Press, 1998), pp. 76–7.
38. Burton Paulu, *British Broadcasting: Radio and Television in the United Kingdom* (Minneapolis: University of Minnesota Press, 1956), p. 209.
39. Minutes of the Home Service Board, Dec 1939, quoted in Asa Briggs, *The History of Broadcasting in the United Kingdom, Vol. 3: The War of Words* (London: Oxford University Press, 1970), p. 113.
40. Minutes of the Home Service Board, December 1939, quoted in Briggs, p. 113.
41. Louis MacNeice, *Christopher Columbus: A Radio Play* (1944; London: Faber and Faber, 1963), p. 89.
42. MacNeice, *Christopher Columbus*, p. 89.
43. Two of the most famous instances came at the very end of the war in the films *Way to The Stars* (Anthony Asquith, 1945) and *A Matter of Life and Death* (Michael Powell and Emeric Pressburger, 1946). MacNeice's play shares aspects of its execution with the poem 'The

Casualty' which treats the same subject matter in a similar manner. See Louis MacNeice, *Collected Poems* (London: Faber and Faber, 2007), pp. 237–40.
44 It is surely this play he refers to in a later collection on parable: 'I myself have had several shots at this but only once, I think, to my own satisfaction.' Louis MacNeice, *Varieties of Parable: The Clark Lectures 1963* (Cambridge: Cambridge University Press, 1965), p. 9.
45 MacNeice, *The Dark Tower,* p. 22.
46 MacNeice, *The Dark Tower,* p. 21.
47 Quoted in Donald Mitchell, ed., *Letters from a Life: The Selected Letters and Diaries of Benjamin Britten 1913–1976, Vol. 2, 1939–45* (London: Faber and Faber, 1991), p. 1289.
48 Quoted in John Haffenden, *William Empson: Against the Christians* (Oxford: Oxford University Press, 2006), p. 23.
49 Smith, 'Castle on the Air', p. 88.
50 Several works on radio drama and its potential written by BBC producers were available to MacNeice, e.g. Gordon Lea, *Radio Drama and How to Write It* (London: George Allen and Unwin, 1926); Val Gielgud, *How to Write Broadcast Plays* (London: Hurst and Blackett, 1932); Lance Sieveking, *The Stuff of Radio* (London: Cassell, 1934).
51 Sean Street, *A Concise History of British Radio: 1922–2002* (Tiverton: Kelly, 2002), p. 39. See also: Tim Crook, *Radio Drama Theory and Practice* (London: Routledge, 1999); Andrew Crisell, *Understanding Radio* (2nd edition; London: Methuen, 1994) and Dermot Rattigan, *Theatre of Sound: Radio and the Dramatic Imagination* (Dublin: Carysfort Press, 2002).
52 Quoted in Street, p. 37.
53 See also Louis MacNeice, 'Scripts Wanted!', in *BBC Yearbook, 1947* (London: British Broadcasting Company, 1947), pp. 25–8 and the later 'A Plea for Sound', in *BBC Quarterly* 8(Autumn, 1953), pp. 129–35.
54 Valentin Iremonger in *The Bell*, quoted in Robyn Marsack, *The Cave of Making: The Poetry of Louis MacNeice* (Oxford: Oxford University Press, 1982), p. 83.
55 MacNeice, *Christopher Columbus*, p. 7.
56 MacNeice, *Christopher Columbus*, p. 7. Unacknowledged detractors of radio are alluded to in his article 'Scripts Wanted!' while Coulton identifies several contemporary articles and writers whose comments seem to undermine the notion that radio might be a serious medium (Coulton, pp. 95–6).
57 MacNeice, *Christopher Columbus*, p. 9.
58 MacNeice, *Christopher Columbus*, p. 12.
59 MacNeice, *The Dark Tower,* p. 12.
60 MacNeice, *Christopher Columbus*, p. 15.
61 Coulton, p. 137.
62 MacNeice, *Autumn Sequel*, p. 28.
63 MacNeice, *Autumn Sequel*, p. 28.
64 MacNeice, *Christopher Columbus*, p. 9.
65 MacNeice, *Christopher Columbus*, p. 9.
66 MacNeice, *Christopher Columbus*, p.10.
67 MacNeice, *Christopher Columbus*, p. 10.
68 MacNeice, *Autumn Sequel,* p. 29.
69 MacNeice, *Christopher Columbus*, p. 13.
70 MacNeice, *Christopher Columbus*, p. 13.
71 MacNeice, *The Dark Tower,* p. 13.
72 MacNeice, *The Dark Tower,* p. 15.
73 MacNeice, *The Dark Tower,* p. 15.
74 E.g. Cecil Day Lewis, *A Hope for Poetry* (1934; Oxford: Basil Blackwell, 1947); Geoffrey Grigson, ed., *The Arts To-Day* (London: John Land, 1935).

'The better it is written the worse it is': Storm Jameson on Popular Fiction and the Political Novel
Kristin Ewins

Throughout her long career the prolific novelist, political journalist and wartime President of English PEN, Margaret Storm Jameson, staunchly defended the importance of a writer's ethical outlook for the overall quality of his or her work.[1] Jameson's emphasis on what precise writerly characteristics made for an ethical aesthetics changed over time; however, she formulated most of the central questions about the relationship between form and subject matter for political fiction in the 1930s. In a 1932 review of Q.D. Leavis's *Fiction and the Reading Public* (1932) for A.R. Orage's *New English Weekly*, Jameson adopted Leavis's claim that 'bad fiction has a direct influence on society through the minds of its readers'[2] as a starting point for outlining the core of her own ethical aesthetics:

> If a novel is not [social criticism] it is nothing much. Critics readily assume that if a novel is well-written it must be a good novel. But if its effect is to persuade its readers to accept a cheap nasty view of life (as for instance that to live well all that they need is a car and a handbook of Freudian first principles) then the better it is written the worse it is. This is not because fiction should be moral (to use a time-saving formula), but because by no means can fiction avoid a moral effect.[3]

There is a conflict between political and aesthetic considerations for the literary critic, and this highlights the central antithesis between politics and 'art' running through so much of Jameson's criticism. Fiction-writing is political business, and without an element of 'social criticism' – that is, criticism of society's 'false and decaying values'[4] – a novel cannot be 'good' however 'well-written'. If somewhat uneasily at times, Jameson maintained that aesthetic considerations were secondary to political ones in assessing literature and art, and that a 'well-written' novel which purveys a degenerate view of life may be worse than any other precisely in virtue of being well-crafted ('The better it is written the worse it is'). We may want to question Jameson's underlying assumption that the moral effect of a novel is something homogenous that is shared by all readers, and indeed that it is, somehow if only partly, independent of form: that the form of the novel takes us in a different direction to its moral effect. In fact, this implication may well have been a consequence of the polemic urgency of Jameson's review, and certainly did not exclude a deep commitment to the possibility of finding an alternative form, one which would, incidentally, be the most appropriate for the politically-minded fiction she herself wrote.

In another review for the *New English Weekly*, also published in 1932, she responded to a reader's letter that had complained that she made 'far too much fuss about the way a book is written. "So long as the matter is all right, the form – in a novel – doesn't matter"'. Jameson clarified her conception of form by first rejecting the reader's sentiment, and then by emphasising the interrelation of form and content: 'It may sometimes be convenient to speak of form as though it were something apart from the writer's attitude, so long as we know what we are doing and do not, by the mere act of treating it separately, come to think of it as a separable quality.'[5] Here, the question was not to give priority to content over form, but to highlight the complex relationship between them: that is, although Jameson often emphasised content, the form always remained an integral and essential part of the whole. So even when, in 1970, Jameson maintained the centrality of content ('I believe that the raison d'être, or excuse, of fiction is and must be, in the first place, its content'), she still emphasised the need for form to be 'precise and evocative' and, most of all, accessible: 'the novelist's language must be a medium in common use in his time.'[6]

I propose to investigate in this essay how Jameson arrived at her most significant contribution to the theory of the political novel, the article 'Documents' which appeared in the short-lived radical monthly *Fact* in July 1937, and how her theorising about political fiction in contradistinction to, on the one hand, the popular novel and, on the other, modernist experimental works, informed her own literary writing. First, I will trace Jameson's development of an ethical aesthetics by examining some of her journalistic comments and reviews, and outline her relationship to the Leavisite critical project of educating the reader. I will then explore how Jameson situated the authentic socialist writer in the context of contemporary political writing. This discussion will concentrate on 'Documents' and elucidate the significance of Jameson's two key terms 'fact' and 'document', which she made much use of in developing the aesthetic guidelines she believed should inform the political novel of the future. Finally, I will suggest some ways in which Jameson put theory into practice in her own fiction.

An Ethical Aesthetics: Educating Readers

Jameson's aesthetics ran counter to contemporary critical norms. In the passage from her review referred to earlier, she deliberately placed herself at a distance from the critical establishment, the 'critics', instead aligning herself with the more controversial critical project driven by the Leavises at

Cambridge. Jameson's awareness of her esoteric critical position was evident, for instance, in a note she attached to one of her Leavisite essays: 'Intending to be unkind a friend said to me the other day: "Let's see, you're the Leavises' only disciple outside Cambridge, aren't you?" I don't know whether they would have been pleased. I was.'[7] Again, in the opening paragraphs of her review of Q.D. Leavis's *Fiction and the Reading Public*, Jameson firmly maintained that the book 'should be in the hands of every serious writer, every self-respecting critic, and every teacher of English'.[8] Leavis later returned the compliment with an unusually mellow 1935 review of Jameson's novel *Love in Winter* (1935) for *Scrutiny*. Having criticised the snobbishness and pretentiousness of Naomi Mitchison's *We Have Been Warned* (1935), Leavis went on to praise Jameson's plain and unassuming style:

> Miss Jameson too has set out to give a cross-section of contemporary society, and the comparison [...] is entirely in her favour. She shows how much can be done by observing and composing with nothing more showy than stubborn honesty, humility and the sensitiveness that goes with solidity of character.[9]

The clearest point of connection with the Leavisite project was Jameson's belief in the possibility and desirability of educating readers' taste. In her essay 'Culture and Environment', for instance, on the book of that name by F.R. Leavis and Denys Thompson, she echoed their analysis of a decaying culture: 'Back we come to the same place. Create awareness, train sensibility, educate taste. A man trained to use his mind will – use it'.[10] Jameson adopted the creed of the subtitle of Leavis's and Thompson's book, 'The Training of Critical Awareness', and emphasised that education of the ordinary person was essential if modern society were to resist the dangers of corruption by advertising, cheap fiction and unsound political propaganda.

Although Jameson followed the Leavises closely on these points, her emphasis on the political causes of cultural decay and the demise of moral values had a more radical edge. Writing in 1932, in a Leavisite vein, Jameson maintained strongly that literary taste depends on economic and social circumstances, and that when taste is bad, society is at fault:

> If you give me a child to bring up as I choose I promise you to breed in him a taste for sound fiction and a distaste for what is bad and facile. But if you take him from me at five, educate him shortly and poorly, bind him to the industrial machine, deafen him with a million tongues all at once making the same worthless and lying statement – expect nothing better than that he will look to the gutter press for truth and to the bestseller for literature.[11]

The underlying assumption that it is clear-cut what is 'sound' and what is 'bad and facile' cannot be ignored, a point on which, of course, the Leavises have often been taken to task. Be that as it may, Jameson's identification of poor education as the cause of infected minds led her to locate the origins of poor taste in the class system. In the essay on the arms race she wrote for a pacifist collection in 1934, *Challenge to Death*, Jameson levelled her criticism at the people at the extremes of the class system as much as the system itself:

> We have two socially irresponsible classes – an upper and a lower, a rich, spending class and a poor, machine-serving class, both relieved from the *necessity* of taking any interest in the direction of society [...] Their mere existence side by side is a source of bad taste in books, films.[12]

However, later in the same essay she challenged the idea that there were personal attributes that were inherent in a person's class, such as his or her educational abilities, and argued that a truly egalitarian education was the only solution to the problems of a decaying culture:

> We should have to educate each child according to its real abilities, and in deciding whether they should be trained with a view to manual or intellectual labours we could not take into account the accident of its father being a company director or a coal-heaver. We waste a great deal of good human material by confusing real biological inequalities with artificially-created ones.[13]

Again, in 'Culture and Environment' Jameson praised F.R. Leavis's pamphlet *How to Teach Reading*, which had been written as a response to Ezra Pound's *How to Read*:

> When the cultural standards of a country have decayed you cannot mend them by slashing at the top of the tree as it rots. The root cause of the trouble lies in the fact that no provision is made at any stage of our educational system for developing critical sensibility.[14]

But not only the critics, or the system, were at fault in failing to recognise the moral peril in which readers and potential readers were placed. Jameson argued that readers were also to blame for the decay of culture. In a provocative article with the title question 'Why Do *You* Read Novels?' Jameson addressed the average reader with a direct reproof:

> [You] read novels merely to quiet your nerves [...] taking wilfully into your system the most potent of all drugs [...] to be got cheaply or for the

asking – from public and circulating libraries, Book Clubs, magazines; in unregulated and increasing quantity.[15]

Jameson referred approvingly in this article to Q.D. Leavis: her analogy between popular fiction and drugs and her disdain for the providers of mass culture (libraries, book clubs and magazines) openly endorsed Leavis's similar antipathies and analogies in *Fiction and the Reading Public*. However, as Catherine Clay has noted, this article also provided Jameson with a chance to depart from Leavis's position, or at least to express her scepticism about its viability:

> Mrs Leavis thinks that an organised critical minority could restore fiction to a decent dignity. I do not believe it. A society gets the fiction it deserves; social rottenness breeds rotten fiction as it breeds slums, Hollywood, war, and disease.[16]

The symbiotic relationship between cultural production and social decay that Jameson identified takes us back to her concern about the moral and political impact of literature. Concluding her review of Leavis's book in the same year as this article was written, and for the same journal, Jameson returned to this sceptical view, albeit regretfully. She concluded that it would be 'barely possible' for 'a critical minority, aware of the dangers [to] do something to counteract them'.[17]

Resisting the Avant-garde

As much as Jameson despaired of popular novels, she had as little patience for modernist experimental texts, with a few notable exceptions, including those of W.H. Auden.[18] In the case of popular fiction, she disliked the falsity of the view of life it perpetuated; when it came to more avant-garde writing, it was the lack of connection with human values and human reality that particularly perturbed her. However, it was not interest in form in itself that Jameson criticised, but rather obsession with form for its own sake, divorced from moral or political effect. In a firm rejection of 'art for art's sake', she maintained in her 1932 essay 'The Craft of the Novelist' that 'there is no such thing as a book or a picture existing apart from human terms of reference, since a man made it and a man receives it'.[19] Even when writing a satirical account of men's relationship with women, she could not resist observing that

> too many novels are written for no purpose at all. There is no such thing as pure art in the novel, though young men beginning criticism like to

think that there may be, and commonly select for praise some rather old-fashioned French novel – in a translation – as an example of pure art.[20]

Note the jibe at the inexperienced critics, all 'young men', upbraided for their pretentious and misplaced praise.

When a year later Jameson published the closest she ever came to a sustained modernist narrative – the moving interior monologue of a day in the poverty-struck life of a kept woman, *A Day Off* (1933) – she pulled off a model example of the type of fiction she sought: one in which form furthers social critique. This was not how she saw the work at the time. Even though she later refer to this novella as 'perhaps the only genuinely imaginative book I have written',[21] using 'imaginative' in the narrow context of avant-garde experimentalism, in the 1930s she soon rejected her attempt as 'no good' and lacking in '*social significance*' [Jameson's italics].[22] She reconceived her aesthetic project as one apparently closer to conventional forms of realism.

It is true that, as Chiara Briganti has suggested, Jameson's 'political commitment' in the 1930s fuelled a different kind of 'formal experimentation', in which she drew, for instance, on the panoramic perspective used by the documentary film makers.[23] And in her seminal biography, Jennifer Birkett has demonstrated the self-conscious investment in form and the stylistic complexities of Jameson's writing: what Birkett calls her 'stylised realism', in which 'the forms of 1930s social documentary, fiction and film, were married to the different modernities of Stendhal, Flaubert, Baudelaire and the Symbolistes, Giraudoux, Eliot, and Auden'.[24] Birkett's exceptional reading of Jameson's engagement with European culture suggests some of the different influences which contributed to Jameson's esoteric aesthetic and writing. However, well into her seventies Jameson remained critical of interwar avant-garde attempts to reflect political crises in language and painting; that is, their foregrounding of form at the expense of subject-matter:

> The one belief – or prejudice – I hold firmly is that insecurity and disorder are not most intimately expressed by disordered language, just as I do not believe that Picasso's *Guernica* offered a very profound or evocative vision of terror. My strong instinct is that a powerful emotional charge is conveyed by a prose of extreme nakedness and dryness better, with more authority, than by any other.[25]

The passage rehearses an antithesis between politics and formally experimental and self-conscious art, which parallels her comments about the antithesis between a political outlook and popular fiction. Her criticism of Surrealist tenets is marked not only by the rejection of 'disordered language' and

Picasso's abstract and symbolic rendering of the anti-Republican destruction of Guernica, but more specifically by the idea that any faithful treatment of the world in art must be invested by a personal perspective. The passage also shows the integrity of Jameson's aesthetic convictions. She refused to approve of Picasso's painting of the obliteration of Guernica despite the attractiveness of his political perspective: the painting had been commissioned by the Spanish Republican government for the 1937 World's Fair in Paris.[26]

In the same article, Jameson proceeded to argue for the representational power of language as a challenge to avant-garde writing. James Joyce emerges as one of the more obvious targets, in, for instance, her claim that 'Language is in varying degrees, but unavoidably, representational; all attempts to overleap the bounds thus set to its uses land the bold would-be violater in confusion and non-sense, or in bombast'.[27] At the same time, Jameson is sensitive to the limitations of linguistic precision: 'Poets – even a novelist or two – have dreamed of a one-to-one correspondence between language and reality. It doesn't and cannot exist.' Nonetheless, she affirmed that 'morally, sensually, ethically, aesthetically, the writer cannot afford the mental relief of admitting to himself that there is an unbridgeable gap between language, written or thought, and reality, exterior or interior'.[28]

More importantly for Jameson's ethical aesthetics, she pre-empted criticism of the deceptively plain and dry style of writing she had just proposed in the first passage I quoted, and emphasised its flexibility: 'A prose of extreme dryness and nakedness – well, yes. But at the same time a prose supple enough to turn and twist with the novelist through the labyrinth of his own mind and heart and the appalling confusion outside.'[29] This was the type of language that would, arguably, have the power to contain both Jameson's political and aesthetic priorities. It should be pointed out that the very 'dryness and nakedness' of the style Jameson proposed made it as formally self-conscious and, at times, complex as avant-garde writing which may strike us more immediately as experimental.

'Documents' and 'Facts'

In the 1930s Jameson's solution to the problem of a rotten society, disengaged critics and pretentious writers and artists was to develop the outlines of a new kind of political fiction. Her 1937 article for *Fact*, 'Documents', is a major examination of what can be done with a genuinely left-wing fiction without sacrificing the demands of form and artistic integrity. Samuel Hynes has described it as 'the first theory of documentary as a literary form', aimed at 'the creation of a great socialist literature',[30] and it has tended to be discussed more than most of Jameson's writing. The essay was published as the first of four studies of literary genre in a themed issue under the general title 'Writing in Revolt'.[31] Paralleling Ralph Fox's call in *The Novel and the People* (1937) for a 'new realism',[32] Jameson attempted to define 'a new literature', which, in her view, unlike 'proletarian literature', would be truly socialist:

> I believe we should do well to give up talking about proletarian literature and talk about socialist literature instead – and mean by it writing concerned with the lives of men and women in a world which is changing and being changed. A socialist must be intimately concerned with this change; he must be struggling continually to understand it.[33]

The problem with 'proletarian literature' was, Jameson argued, that it focused on the working classes without necessarily exploring the genesis of the injustices that they suffer:

> The use of the term 'proletarian novel' suggests, quite falsely, that socialist literature ought to concern itself only or mainly with working-class life. In fact, a novel about a Lord Invernairn, written from full insight into what this man actually is doing, a novel which exposed him, laid him open, need not bring on to the stage a single one of the people who do not exist for him as human beings. It would still be socialist literature.[34]

Again, it was the moral effect of the novel aided by a deceptively simple form which counted for Jameson. She was fiercely critical of the middle-class writer who self-consciously chose to live in the slums and fetishised their grim conditions instead of understanding what had created them. Her specific target was George Orwell, whom she somewhat unfairly mocked as the middle-class writer straight out of Kensington who had just sold off all his possessions to go and live the authentic working-class life. Jameson criticised this type of writer for his overriding 'curiosity about his [own] feelings': 'What things I am seeing for the first time! What smells I am enduring! There is the woman raking ashes with her hands and here I am watching her!' Jameson was wary of explicitly depicting emotional reactions, although it is unclear whether she considered this a purely aesthetic issue, or whether she believed it would hinder the capacity for a socialist novel to engage with the task of rendering social reality:

> The first thing a socialist writer has to realize is that there is no value in the emotions, the spiritual writhings, started in him by the sight, smell, and

touch of poverty. The emotions are no doubt unavoidable. There is no need to record them. Let him go and pour them down the drain.[35]

What Jameson was proposing was not a lack of empathy, but rather a stripping away of self-consciousness and emotions coloured by prejudice. Instead, Jameson privileged the 'fact', that core bit of information which should be the focus of the writer's well-placed perspective on a topic:

> As the photographer [of documentary film] does, so must the writer keep himself out of the picture while working ceaselessly to present the *fact* from a striking (poignant, ironic, penetrating, significant) angle. The narrative must be sharp, compressed, concrete. Dialogue must be short – a seizing of the significant, the revealing word. The emotion should spring directly from the fact. It must not be squeezed from it by the writer, running forward with a 'When I say this, I felt, I suffered, I rejoiced ...' His job is not to tell us what he felt, but to be coldly and industriously presenting, arranging, selecting, discarding from the mass of his material to get the significant detail which leaves no more to be said, and implies everything.[36]

This was the ideal of socialist writing: staying 'out of the picture' as much as possible, while remaining in control of the 'angle' from which to present the material – the 'form' in which the 'fact' is to be presented. Methodologically, Jameson drew on the Leavises' emphasis on the moral responsibility of writers and critics; but her ideas also shared features with Charles Madge's and Tom Harrisson's Mass-Observation project. The first Mass-Observation pamphlet had been published six months earlier in January 1937 and similarly aimed to work out a new method for documenting social reality.[37] Interestingly, Madge and Harrisson developed their methodology in the very same three academic fields that Q.D. Leavis had drawn on in *Fiction and the Reading Public*: 'psychology, anthropology, and sociology.'[38] Jameson's call to the documentary novelist to go to impoverished areas 'for the sake of the *fact*, as a medical student carries out a dissection, and to equip himself, not to satisfy his conscience or to see what effect it has on him',[39] paralleled Madge's and Harrisson's description of Mass-Observation as 'an instrument for collecting facts': 'The availability of the facts will liberate certain tendencies in science, art, and politics, because it will add to the social consciousness of the time.'[40] The title of the magazine in which Jameson's article was published – *Fact* – in itself indicated the importance of 'facts' for the socialist project.

Jameson singled out Ignazio Silone's *Fontamara* (1934) as a novel that managed to present 'facts' unsentimentally and succinctly: 'this tragic, bitter story of a village is extremely funny, and sticks faster in the memory by it.'[41] She proceeded to offer a list of instructions for socialist writers: to cut 'atmosphere', 'the static analysis of feeling, and thought', 'stream of consciousness', 'commentary', 'aesthetic, moral, or philosophic enquiry'. Jameson stipulates that

> we must be field workers in a field no smaller than England, our criticism of values implied in the angle from which we take our pictures. By choosing this detail, this word, rather than another from the mass offered us, we make our criticism, our moral judgements.[42]

This method was subjective, but not personal. It was when the personal interfered that Jameson got agitated. And for Jameson the personal was often connected with a particular class perspective or background. In 'Documents', she criticised the Orwellian writer for failing to rid himself of his privileged class perspective:

> If, as a child, he had escaped from the nursery and been found in some Hoxton backyard he would have been bathed and disinfected and made conscious of having run an awful danger, much as though he had been visiting savages. The mental attitude persists. Breeding will out![43]

This exaggerated example was used by Jameson to illustrate how difficult – near impossible – it was for a writer to shed his or her class background, even though this was necessary for being able to write socialist fiction. In a review of Orwell's *The Road to Wigan Pier* (1937), also for *Fact* and published only two months before 'Documents', Jameson singled out the first part of Orwell's book as a model for socialist writing: 'in the first part of his book he has provided a social document as vivid, bitter, and telling as one could have asked'. However, she went on to criticise the second and reflective part of Orwell's account of a mining village in decline:

> [I]t reveals the width of the gulf, mental and moral, between the public school boy turned Socialist and the socialist worker. George Orwell is far from denying the existence of this gulf. This part of his book is largely concerned with his own flounderings in it. What is significant is that he finds it necessary to give so much time and energy to this personal problem.[44]

The review was decidedly coloured by her own project of defining socialist writing. Nonetheless, although Jameson appreciated Orwell's 'hatred of social injustice' and his attempt 'to bring others of the sinking middle-class into the pack', she is clear about the practical action that must follow: 'it is time we middle-class socialists shut down on our personal problem and devoted our energies to direct action of the sort best suited to us.'[45] *The Road to Wigan Pier* was reviewed alongside *Unemployed Struggles, 1919–1936* (1936) by Wal Hannington and *Smoky Crusade* (1937) by Ralph Fox.[46] In contrast to Orwell's personal reflections, Jameson celebrated Wal Hannington's narrative self-effacement in his book *Unemployed Struggles* as a model narrative:

> His first reference to himself in his book begins: 'I was working at the time in a North London engineering firm'. Maybe he was born there, and learned to talk by making speeches. He doesn't say. And throughout the whole book 'I' only appears in action, leading a raid into a factory or the House of Commons, preparing the details of a hunger march, arguing with employers and Labour leaders.[47]

Class seems to have been an inescapable factor once again: Hannington was a working-class card-carrying Communist. Hannington, then, was in a way true to his class background. On the other hand the Communist writer Ralph Fox, with his *Smoky Crusade*, exemplified for Jameson the pretentious working-class writer who wished he had been born in a middle-class family, 'the clever son of a clever workman':

> [O]ne is free to doubt whether, had he been born in Orwell's class, he would have taken the road to Wigan pier. It seems a great deal more likely that he would have become a liberal-minded scholar with a sincere but academic belief in freedom of opinion. From start to finish he is the centre of this account of his life and activities; he sees himself as a sort of symbol of a cheated and struggling youth.[48]

She critiqued, then, both the self-obsessed proletarian and upper-middle-class writers' bourgeois preoccupation with the self.

Despite her eagerness to abandon the proletarian novel in favour of the socialist novel, the socialist novelists that Jameson seems to praise the most were all proletarian writers, dealing with working-class subjects. Besides Hannington, Jameson recommended Chris Massie's *Flood Light* (1932) and James Hanley's *Ebb and Flood* (1932), of which she gave an exalted combined review in *The New Clarion*:

> What do you want from a novel? […] To be titillated or to escape – if you want nothing else (and nothing less comfortable and consoling) do not trouble to read either of these books. You won't like them – they will disturb without pleasing you; they will force you to look at certain aspects of life instead of turning your back on them and hoping for the best.[49]

Kristin Ewins

The review came out five years before 'Documents'; however, the uncensored version of harsh working-class life that Massie and Hanley produced perfectly fitted the model of the documentary account Jameson came to draw up. She had a special affinity with Hanley and read several drafts of his 1935 novel, *The Furys*. What she admired most about this novel, as she wrote to Hanley in 1934, was its quality as an 'epic of working-class life'.[50] Her own major work of the 1930s – the *Mirror in Darkness* trilogy, originally planned to include five or six books – had an even grander epic scope. Its subject-matter and its treatment looked forward to much of the theory that she outlined in 'Documents'; for instance, it is not confined to a proletarian setting, but cuts across different classes and social milieux to reveal the complex relationships and constellations of events that produce the ills of society. And in the last novel of the trilogy, *None Turn Back* (1936), for instance, we do not see the miners of the General Strike, but see instead the political and social landscape shaping and reflecting the personal interests of a group of people. The novel is about the General Strike, but it does not, as socialist realist fiction would, depict the miners directly. Rather their struggles are revealed through the parallel struggles of their union representatives, suggesting some of the oblique nature of Jameson's political fiction.

The *Mirror in Darkness* Trilogy

In 1933 Jameson complained to her then close friend, the feminist writer Vera Brittain, that

> what with Mrs Leavis and what with Gestalt, I have been educated beyond my intelligence. It's an awful thing but I can't think of a novel to write in 1933 – all the ones I had in a cupboard have got the moth, I find, on taking them down.[51]

Her dissatisfaction with the novels that she had previously planned, and which now seemed outdated and moth-eaten, coincided with her engagement with the Leavisite critical and educational project, and also with an increased political consciousness that grew throughout the 1930s. The next large fiction project on which she embarked was the *Mirror in Darkness* series of novels, tracing the origins of the General Strike of 1926. The trilogy contained the novels *Company Parade* (1934), *Love in Winter* (1935) and *None Turn Back* (1936). Jameson attempted to represent a collective view of the General Strike, in line with contemporary novels such as Gwyn Jones's *Times like These* (1936) and James Barke's *Major Operation* (1936). In a largely appreciative review of the first of the *Mirror in Darkness* novels, *Company Parade*, for *The Spectator*, Graham Greene suggested that Jameson's novel was 'successful in a not very common *genre*, the novel of contemporary history, which subordinates fiction to the interpretation of this period'. Astutely, he picked out '[Jameson's] fastidiousness of phrase and tight emotional control. The dialogue is spare, curt, as necessary to the theme as the dialogue in a good play. There is no hazy writing, no padding, and she has the ability to describe her characters quickly and clearly'.[52] Greene's appreciative comments about Jameson's language matched precisely with Jameson's own call for 'a prose of extreme nakedness and dryness' to which I have already referred.[53]

When in 1936, Jameson came to review Allen Hutt's Marxist account of the condition of England, *This Final Crisis* (1935),[54] she remarked that it was 'the events of the years since May 1926 which have forced me, and others like me, to realize that we cannot resign our political thinking to the leaders of the Labour Party'.[55] The treachery of the Labour leaders during the strike became an important theme in the last of the novels in the trilogy, *None Turn Back*. But while retaining the socialist focus of her comments and reviews, and anticipating the theories she developed in 'Documents', Jameson specifically focused in these novels on the condition of the women.

In the social panorama of the run-up to 1926 in the *Mirror in Darkness* trilogy we have a professional heroine, Hervey Russell, a writer, who has to reconcile professional and political convictions with private pressures: not just the pressures associated with romance, but also with motherhood, divorce, and an operation which will leave her barren. Although the *Mirror in Darkness* trilogy marked a distinct new mode of writing for Jameson, she retained some of the domestic interests which had fuelled her earlier fiction. Jameson's early novels, from 1919 to the beginning of the 1930s, were more exclusively domestic in their outlook. In her reviews of *None Turn Back* and of Jameson's 1936 dystopia of Britain as a fascist state in the near future, *In the Second Year*, for the *Times Literary Supplement*, Leonora Eyles pleaded for Jameson's return first 'to her Yorkshire moors and [...] her memorable pictures of Yorkshire life' and then 'to her Yorkshire shipyards, to real life and real human beings'.[56] But Jameson's concern was precisely with the effects of social injustice on personal lives. So when the workers in *None Turn Back* are betrayed by the General Council of the Trades Union Congress – calling off the strike to save their own skin but with no guarantees for the workers' employment – we come up against the desperate face of an engineer inside the union office, who has just realised his destitution after being called out on strike the day before, even as the General Council were covertly retreating. Some of these characters are admittedly flat – metonymies standing in for the woes of an entire class – but Jameson powerfully depicts the consequences of social events in the reactions of the wives of strikers and trade unionists. We see this, for example, in the vacant eyes of the wife of one of the socialist leaders when she realises that her husband has betrayed the workers ('Her face was paler than usual, her eyes wide open').[57]

Jameson regularly uses the wife's viewpoint to make a political point, about the marginalisation of ordinary individuals in this society, and specifically, of women, who see more than they let on. The fear of how one's wife will react looms large as the defeated strikers return home. And ultimately it is from the home, with its constancy – bookshelves built by an elderly father, 'the chest of drawers Sally had from her mother' – that reassurance and hope come. To make all good, Sally smiles to her husband and says: 'We'll do somehow.'[58]

The female interest in these novels carves out some common ground with the semi-intellectual novels, sometimes called middlebrow, driven by domestic interests and often a romantic main plot, which were especially popular among women in the interwar period. The roots of this genre lay in the bourgeois nineteenth-century novel, and its interest in character and domesticity often met with disdain in left-wing quarters. However, for Jameson it provided some of the tools for a socialist fiction which remained sensitive to a female point of view. She firmly rejected the idea that middlebrow novels were not competent to address crucial political issues. In an unprinted lecture of 1932 in honour of the philosopher and science fiction writer Olaf Stapledon, Jameson defended the place and work of the middlebrow writer. The average novelist had the same value as a 'tolerable thin wine': 'a loyal honest little *vin du pays*, need not disappoint, is not worthless. It would be worthless if it were offered as *premier cru*, or if it were adulterated. As its self, it has a place in life.'[59] Coming as it does from a deeply committed political writer, the comment justified Jameson's own use of the middlebrow mode to radical ends.

The significance of the female perspective may also be seen in Jameson's inclusion – as editor of the same issue of *Fact* in which 'Documents' appeared – of a short story by James Hanley, as an example of documentary fiction. The story, 'Episode', is a grim tale about the desperate and frustrated attempts of the mother in a working-class family to manage the family budget with an unemployed husband, reduced to idleness by continual rejection by employers. With plain descriptive clarity, it presented the uncompromisingly tragic facts from the woman's perspective. Several of the examples in 'Documents' also homed in on the woman's position. One of the most evocative instances emerged in an imagined scene illustrating the complacency of the middle-class writer's perspective:

> The middle-class writer [...] discovers that he does not even know what the wife of a man earning two pounds a week wears, where she buys her food,

what her kitchen looks like to her when she comes into it at six or seven in the morning. It has never happened to him to stand with his hands in greasy water at the sink, with a nagging pain in his back, and his clothes sticking to him [...] he does not know as much as the woman's finger knows when it scrapes the black out of a crack in the table or the corner of the shelf.[60]

In *None Turn Back*, the narrative ends in an even more private space inhabited by a woman: the hospital room in which Hervey is recovering after her operation. The pain of the operation, which 'leaped in her body like a flame, licking at its walls', is the pain of loneliness and isolation, but is also the pain shared with all suffering workers. The tone at the end is romantic and personal, as Hervey thinks back to her husband's concern as he visited the hospital: 'It was no little matter that her second husband did not feel it below his dignity to worry about her when she was ill.'[61] Although the domestic values celebrated at the end of *None Turn Back* are shaken by the operation which has left Hervey barren, she is left with a political and public role in society which is depicted as more important than her domestic role as wife and mother. At the same time, her barrenness is analogous to the abortion of the General Strike itself, producing a barren body politic and throwing doubt on the potency of political action itself.

Later in life, Jameson became critical of her attempts at political fiction in the *Mirror in Darkness* trilogy and other novels written in the mid- to late 1930s. In her autobiography, thirty years later, she would recognise the value of 'the energy spent writing polemics against war and fascism' at that time, while criticising her own attempt at translating her political convictions into fiction: 'Wrong as wrong was the fallacy that political passions I could not ignore had somehow to be pressed directly into my novels'.[62] This dissatisfaction with those of her novels that most directly confronted politics had by that time been growing for many years. It is evident, for instance, in an unpublished list dated 1951 in which Jameson outlined, on the one hand, 'the books I should like to have in print' (these included *A Day Off*) and, on the other, those about which Jameson claimed to be 'indifferent': the *Mirror in Darkness* novels and *In the Second Year*, among others.[63] The changes in Jameson's critical and writerly preferences are part of a process of constant self-questioning and probing of an aesthetics which could encompass the central values of justice and freedom.

Jameson developed her documentary mode of writing in much of the fiction she produced during and just after the Second World War, especially in *Europe to Let* (1940) about a Europe bereft of any value. In later writing, however, she refrained from the direct engagement with political conflict that had shaped her fiction of the mid- and late 1930s. As I have shown, through most of that decade Jameson opposed both popular and avant-garde modes of writing and advocated a content-driven approach, which still, however, depended on literary form. The form she proposed and adopted in her own criticism and fiction was one of deliberate sparsity and directness, but one that crucially evoked deep feeling: the form being essential to the effect of the novel. But the key feature of a successful novelist remained for Jameson his or her political edge. Near the beginning of her autobiography, she summed up this notion: 'all writers who claim to be called "living" must be political in a sense. They must have what the Quakers call a concern to understand what is happening in the world.'[64]

Notes

1. PEN is the acronym for the writers' association Poets, Essayists, Novelists. Margaret Storm Jameson was born in 1891 and died in 1986.
2. Rpt. in Jameson, 'Novels and Novelists', *Civil Journey* (London: Cassell, 1939), p. 81.
3. Jameson, 'Novels and Novelists', pp. 83–4.
4. Jameson, 'Novels and Novelists', p. 81.
5. Jameson, 'Novels and Novelists', pp. 87–8.
6. Jameson, 'A New Language?', *Parthian Words* (London: Collins, 1970), p. 139.
7. Jameson, Introduction, 'Culture and Environment', *Civil Journey*, p. 115.
8. Jameson, 'Novels and Novelists', p. 81.
9. Q.D. Leavis, 'Lady Novelists and the Lower Orders', *Scrutiny* 4 (1935), p. 117.
10. Jameson, 'Culture and Environment', p. 124.
11. Jameson, 'Why Do *You* Read Novels?', *The New Clarion* (11 June 1932), p. 12.
12. Jameson, 'In the End', in Storm Jameson, ed., *Challenge to Death* (London: Constable, 1934), p. 324.
13. Jameson, 'In the End', pp. 324–5.
14. Jameson, 'Culture and Environment', pp. 116–17.
15. Jameson, 'Why Do *You* Read Novels?', p. 12.
16. Catherine Clay, 'Storm Jameson's Journalism 1913–33', in Jennifer Birkett and Chiara Briganti, eds, *Margaret Storm Jameson: Writing in Dialogue* (Newcastle: Cambridge Scholars Publishing, 2007), p. 49; Jameson, 'Why Do *You* Read Novels?', p. 12.
17. Jameson, 'Novels and Novelists', p. 84.
18. See especially Jennifer Birkett's 'A Fictional Function: Storm Jameson and W.H. Auden', *English* (Summer 2007), pp. 171–86; and *Margaret Storm Jameson: A Life* (Oxford: Oxford University Press, 2009), pp. 7–8, p. 146.
19. Jameson, 'The Craft of the Novelist', *Civil Journey*, p. 55.
20. Jameson, 'Man the Helpmate', in Mabel Ulrich, ed., *Man, Proud Man* (London: Hamish Hamilton, 1932), p. 120.
21. Jameson, *Journey from the North: Autobiography of Storm Jameson*, 2 vols (London: Virago, 1969–70), vol. 1, p. 301.
22. Jameson, *Journey from the North*, vol. 1, p. 300.
23. Chiara Briganti, 'Mirroring the Darkness: Storm Jameson and the Collective Novel', in *Margaret Storm Jameson: Writing in Dialogue*, p. 72.
24. Birkett, *Margaret Storm Jameson: A Life*, p. 4.
25. Jameson, 'A New Language?', p. 137.

26 Exposition Internationale des Arts et Techniques dans la Vie Moderne.
27 Jameson, 'A New Language?', p. 137.
28 Jameson, 'A New Language?', p. 138.
29 Jameson, 'A New Language?', p. 138.
30 Samuel Hynes, *The Auden Generation: Literature and Politics in England in the 1930s* (London: Bodley Head, 1976), p. 270.
31 It was reprinted two years later in Jameson's collection of essays, *Civil Journey*, as 'New Documents'.
32 Ralph Fox, *The Novel and the People* (London: Lawrence and Wishart, 1937), p. 34.
33 Jameson, 'Documents', *Fact* (July 1937), p. 9.
34 Jameson, 'Documents', p. 10.
35 Jameson, 'Documents', p. 12.
36 Jameson, 'Documents', p. 15.
37 Charles Madge and Tom Harrisson, *Mass-Observation*, Series One (London: F. Muller, 1937), pp. 10–11.
38 Madge and Harrisson, p. 35.
39 Jameson, 'Documents', p. 13.
40 Madge and Harrisson, p. 47.
41 Jameson, 'Documents', p. 16.
42 Jameson, 'Documents', pp. 16–17.
43 Jameson, 'Documents', p. 13.
44 Jameson, 'Socialists Born and Made', Review of *The Road to Wigan Pier* by George Orwell, *Fact* (May 1937), p. 87.
45 Jameson, 'Socialists Born and Made', p. 87.
46 George Orwell, *The Road to Wigan Pier* (London: Victor Gollancz, 1937); Wal Hannington, *Unemployed Struggles, 1919–1936* (London: Lawrence and Wishart, 1936); and Ralph Fox, *Smoky Crusade* (London: The Hogarth Press, 1937).
47 Jameson, 'Socialists Born and Made', p. 88.
48 Jameson, 'Socialists Born and Made', p. 89.
49 Jameson, 'No Escape: Two Books which Keep to the Facts', Review of *Flood Light* by Chris Massie and *Ebb and Flood* by James Hanley, *The New Clarion* (1 October 1932), p. 391.
50 Letter from Jameson to James Hanley, 20 July 1934, 920 HAN/4/6, Liverpool Records Office.
51 Letter from Jameson to Vera Brittain, 20 December 1932, Incoming Correspondence, Vera Brittain Archive, McMaster University, Hamilton, Ontario, Canada.
52 Graham Greene, Review of *Company Parade* by Storm Jameson, *The Spectator* (20 April 1934), p. 634.
53 Jameson, 'A New Language?', p. 137.
54 Allen Hutt, *This Final Crisis* (London: Victor Gollancz, 1935).
55 Jameson, 'Crisis', Review of *This Final Crisis* by Allen Hutt, *Left Review* (January 1936), p. 156.
56 Leonora Eyles, 'A Second General Strike', Review of *In the Second Year*, *Times Literary Supplement* (1 February 1936), p. 92; Leonora Eyles, Review of *None Turn Back*, *Times Literary Supplement* (29 August 1936), p. 695.
57 Jameson, *None Turn Back* (London: Cassell, 1936), p. 311.
58 Jameson, *None Turn Back*, pp. 311–13.
59 Jameson, Lecture in Honour of Olaf Stapledon, Storm Jameson Papers, Harry Ransom Humanities Research Center, The University of Texas at Austin, p. 4.
60 Jameson, 'Documents', p. 10.
61 Jameson, *None Turn Back*, pp. 315–18.

62 Jameson, *Journey from the North*, vol. 1, p. 344.
63 Jameson, Miscellaneous Notes, 1951, Storm Jameson Papers, Harry Ransom Humanities Research Center, The University of Texas at Austin.
64 Jameson, *Journey from the North*, vol. 1, p. 12.

'Hard as the metal of my gun': Communism, Masculinity and John Cornford's Poetry of the Will[1]

Stan Smith

John Cornford, who died on the Cordoba front in December 1936, is most frequently seen, by both enthusiasts and detractors, as a loyal Communist cadre, subscribing unequivocally to the Party orthodoxy on the situation in Spain. Yet in his most powerful poem, 'Full Moon at Tierz: Before the Storming of Huesca', there is a significant hesitation, focused by a reference to the Seventh Congress of the Comintern. A close scrutiny of this poem, of letters, and a 'Political Report' he wrote from Spain, and an examination of some of his pre-Spain political writings, indicate a more complex picture, and suggest that he had considerable reservations about Party policy, particularly in relation to the 'Popular Front' strategy, and to Communist dealings with other movements in the Republican camp.

The Test

'All presented their lives', wrote W.H. Auden in his 1937 pamphlet poem *Spain*,[2] of the young men who flocked to the aid of the Spanish Republic in the wake of Franco's rebellion on 17 July 1936. John Lehmann, co-editor of the influential anthology *Poems for Spain*,[3] which appeared in 1939, recalled in his 1955 autobiography that in Spain 'everything, all our fears, our confused hopes and beliefs, our half-formulated theories and imaginings, veered and converged towards its testing and its opportunity, like steel filings that slide towards a magnet suddenly put near them'.[4] Subsequently, however, Lehmann reached the conclusion, along with many of his contemporaries, that the Spanish War 'dragged us all deeper into the morass of ideological conflict, putting to the sharpest test the idealism that the advance of fascism in Central Europe had awakened in us'.[5]

Lehmann's concept of a test recalls Christopher Isherwood's declared conviction in *Lions and Shadows*, first published in 1938, that his generation, which was too young to serve in the Great War, had felt from the start the need for some personal test of manhood, in 'a complex of terrors and longings connected with the idea "War"':

> 'War', in this purely neurotic sense, meant The Test. The Test of your courage, of your maturity, of your sexual prowess: 'Are you really a Man?'

Subconsciously, I believe, I longed to be subjected to this test; but I also dreaded failure.[6]

For Isherwood's generation, as for that a decade younger, Spain was the first instalment of this 'Test'.[7] It soon became apparent, however, that a crucial part of such a testing for the liberal intellectual was the struggle with one's conscience to achieve what Auden's poem notoriously dubbed 'conscious acceptance of guilt in the necessary murder', reluctant but willed acquiescence in the brutality that characterises all civil wars, viciously accentuated in this instance by the class and cultural antagonisms of a country torn in the 1930s between modernity and reaction. 'Our generation', Stephen Spender, Lehmann's co-editor on *Poems for Spain*, recalled half a century later, 'was conscripted into politics by Hitler', more or less innocently accepting 'the Marxist interpretation of history' and believing that 'Communism would lead to the freedom of oppressed people, to a world of social justice, and to a depoliticised egalitarian anarchist utopia'.[8] In 1951, looking back on the thirties in his autobiographical Cold War *apologia pro vita sua*, *World Within World*, Spender had already admitted that a major part of his impulsion towards Communism, as a young bourgeois leftist, was a desire to expunge his class guilt:

> Communism [...] seemed to offer a way out of my dilemma. It suggested to me that after all I was not myself. I was simply a product of my bourgeois circumstances. By 'going over to the proletariat' and entering a different set of circumstances I could become another kind of social projection. I would be 'on the side of history' and not 'rejected' by it, like one of the disused mines in Auden's early poems.[9]

Auden himself, who subsequently pleaded a similar political naivety, chose to fall silent after returning from Spain, explaining, later, that at the time progressive writers like himself felt compelled to defend the bad against the worst, but that 'Nobody I know who went to Spain during the Civil War who was not a dyed-in-the-wool Stalinist came back with his illusions intact'.[10] The anonymous *TLS* reviewer of *Poems for Spain* in 1939 registered the nature of these writers' liberal dilemma:

> The tragic conflict in Spain cannot be evaded by the modern poet. Whether or not it compels him to direct expression, it must haunt his mind with painful questions and torture his imagination. For here, as in a theatre but with the appalling realism of indiscriminate slaughter, the discord at the heart of our civilization is nakedly displayed.[11]

But, in the reviewer's opinion, what 'makes the conflict so peculiarly tragic' is that, 'believing that in supporting the Spanish republic they are defending the very life-principle of civilization', these writers found themselves required to use 'weapons that inevitably deny the very values they wish to affirm'.[12] This is not the place to go over yet again the complex amalgam of faith, illusion and self-delusion, credulity and *Realpolitik*, idealism and cynicism, that characterised the international response to the Spanish Civil War. What I want to revisit, rather, is the fraught encounter with Spanish realities of one dedicated and talented young poet, who was prepared to and did in fact die in taking that 'Test'.

Calculated Acts

One of the writers the *TLS* reviewer singled out from *Poems for Spain* was John Cornford, whose poetry, he observed, was 'written by the will rather than from the sensibility […] the calculated acts of a fighter determined in vindicating his creed to be "invincible as the strong sun, / Hard as the metal of my gun"'.[13]

Rupert John Cornford, the son of a distinguished Cambridge academic family, christened in honour of that earlier poetic war casualty, his parents' friend, Rupert Brooke, joined the Communist Party of Great Britain while still at Cambridge University, in 1935. He died on the Cordoba front a day after his twenty-first birthday, on 28 December 1936. Cornford is usually seen as an aggressively orthodox Communist, a posture, it could be argued, maintained partly out of guilt at his privileged and therefore suspect class origins, a stick which the British Communist Party regularly used in the 1930s to beat dissident intellectuals back into conformity with whatever was the current Party line. Yet Cornford's major poem, 'Full Moon at Tierz: Before the Storming of Huesca',[14] is riven by the contradictions of the poet's subject-position. In the idiom of its time, it speaks of Spain as the place where 'our testing has begun'. But it also records that such testing is a matter not only of personal courage in risking one's life in battle. It also involves an inner struggle to overcome personal doubts, reservations and uncertainties, what the poem calls the 'private battle with my nerves', a 'battle' to compel oneself to accept in practice what intellectually one might dispute, in the name of Party discipline.[15]

'Full Moon at Tierz' in fact discloses a more complicated, less doctrinaire reality than that of the public manifestos and pronouncements with which it might be associated, and which are echoed in its closing lines, and it is this very complexity which contributes to its value as a work of literature transcending its polemic origins. The 'testing' announced by the full moon rising over friend and foe alike on the bare hills of Aragon is not only a test of physical courage in the fight with an external and ubiquitous fascism. It refers also to an internal moral struggle with one's bourgeois self, to maintain loyalty to the Party amidst misgivings about its policies and practice.

Such a dilemma was revealed in a letter of Cornford's from the Aragon front to his lover, his fellow Communist Margot Heinemann, written over several days between 16 and 30 August 1936,[16] in which he expressed a new-found sense of solidarity with 'German comrades' in his unit. It was, he says, 'The luckiest accident of the whole war […] that put me in touch with the German comrades', amidst what had previously been 'the same loneliness and isolation as the first term in a new school, without the language and without any kind of distraction of something to do'. 'All the revolutionary enthusiasm was bled out me', he continued, until he met this 'splendid lot', who have 'treated me with a quite extraordinary personal kindness; and at last I can live in the present, get outside of my own mind'.[17]

If, however, he was 'never more glad of anything in my life than the accident which threw me together with them', he felt compelled to report to his ultra-orthodox comrade, almost as if seeking absolution, that 'Four of them are ex-members of the party; one still a member', adding that they had left the KPD 'because they genuinely believe the C.I. [Communist International] has deserted the revolution'.[18] 'Partly, perhaps', he added by way of exoneration, 'it is the uprootedness of emigrants'. His own reluctance to contest their views is explained, a little evasively, on grounds of ignorance: 'I do not know enough of the Spanish position to argue with them successfully.' However, a kind of bravado confidence is restored in the assertion: 'But I am beginning to find out how much the Party and the International have become flesh and blood of me. Even when I can put forward no rational argument, I feel that to cut adrift from the Party is the beginning of political suicide.'[19]

If Cornford really had no doubts, of course, such a cutting adrift would have been quite literally unthinkable. It is a significantly ambivalent note towards the close of a long and variously restarted letter, particularly in that intellectually unprincipled antithesis of 'no rational argument' and 'political suicide'. The strategic position of this particular revelation suggests a deeper disturbance than it will actually admit. The struggle with one's nerves requires the uncertain self to be disciplined into the iron resolve of the unquestioning cadre, even if there is 'no rational argument'. These paragraphs almost seem like an appeal to his hard-line lover for ratification in one direction or another.

The strain of such an inner conflict is apparent in the paradoxical fusion of solidarity and solitude in a single line at the heart of 'Full Moon at Tierz': 'Now with my Party, I stand quite alone.'[20] In the midst of all this enforced solidarity, it is the loneliness which persists. This is the subject steeling himself to a commitment that remains abstract and hortatory, a wish rather than a reality. A hesitant and solitary being wills himself, in a kind of prayer to an absent Marxian deity, not to lose his faith, to be a good Communist:

> Then let my private battle with my nerves,
> The fear of pain whose pain survives,
> The love that tears me by the roots,
> The loneliness that claws my guts,
> Fuse in the welded front our fight preserves.[21]

The poem's closing exhortation, to 'Raise the red flag triumphantly / For Communism and for liberty',[22] is not actually uttered by the poet himself. It is, rather, an imagined affirmation, projected rhetorically into that 'Time future' which the poem's opening section had said 'has no image in space',[23] when 'the workers of all the world' will gather on the plain of Huesca to raise the red flag and 'swear that our dead fought not in vain'.[24] This last formulation recalls the earlier anxious desire to 'prove the agony was not in vain',[25] and suggests deep forebodings about any actual future. The echo of the Italian Communist anthem 'Bandiera Rossa' is a way of strengthening personal resolve, cheering himself up. The poem's real climax comes at the beginning of this last stanza, in the acknowledgment that 'Freedom is an easily spoken word / But facts are stubborn things'.[26] Far from being the utterance of what the *TLS* reviewer called 'a fighter determined in vindicating his creed to be "invincible as the strong sun"', Cornford's poem embodies in its very ambivalences and hesitations a more profound sense of the stress involved in steeling oneself to continue believing in that creed, to be ideologically as 'hard as the metal of my gun'. The ambiguous, deceptive, equivocal light of the moon, not the direct glare of the sun, after all, is what defines the moral space of the poem. This is a poem riddled with doubt, a doubt detectable in the celebration of 'the impartial beauty of the stars' and the indifference of 'the unfeeling sky', or in the references to the 'Crooked [...] road that we must tread', to 'freedom's crooked scars', and to the 'innocent mask' concealing that 'our freedom's swaying in the scales'.[27] The poem's harrowingly dramatic power derives from the way it enacts the very processes by which the isolated individual steels himself rhetorically to sink his ego in a 'welded front'.[28]

A Punishment for Previous Errors

A bad-tempered exchange in the pages of the annual publication *Socialist Register* during 1981–1982 was the site of a revealing squabble over Cornford's literary remains.[29] The dispute was waged between the historian and ex-CP veteran John Saville and the (by his own account) independent socialist, Oxford literary critic Valentine Cunningham, whose *Penguin Book of Spanish Civil War Verse*[30] Saville had attacked in a withering review in the 1981 issue of the annual. Saville, who joined the British Communist Party in 1934 and had been active in its campaign on behalf of Spain, quit the Party in 1956, along with several other distinguished members of the Communist Party Historians Group, to found the *New Reasoner*, one of the first stirrings of an incipient New Left which, to begin with, was predominantly ex-Communist in origin. Saville's review, however, remained loyal to the CPGB line on Spain, and to those figures, such as Harry Pollitt, well-known and clearly fondly recalled by Saville as 'a tough-minded working-class militant with an engaging and warm personality', who had led the Party at the time.[31] It is not my purpose here to adjudicate between these two conflicting but in many ways complementary readings of Cornford's life and commitments. The differences between them have to be read in the context of the different political and cultural agendas from which they emerge. Each contains elements of a partial truth about this complex and conflicted figure, and each in turn witnesses to the historical pressures and what Cunningham calls the 'ideological constraint' exerting a gravitational drag on their interpretations. The apparently irreconcilable disagreement can be resolved if we see that it reflects the strains in Cornford's own conflicted state of mind, symptomatic of the dilemma faced by large sections of the European Left in the 1930s.

Neither commentator disputes the quality of Cornford's poetry, but Cunningham claims that its quality arose despite its author's subscription to the Stalinist orthodoxy of CPGB politics at the time, from which he argues Cornford probably demurred, as evidenced by his joining, on his first visit to Spain, a POUM unit; while Saville seeks to justify those politics and to present Cornford as a convinced adherent of the Party line, and his POUM connection an accident which he rectified on his return to Spain by joining, with Pollitt's encouragement, the Communist-dominated International Brigade.

Both positions seem to me incorrect, or at least incomplete, and both, at the same time, contain a rational kernel. At the centre of the dispute is a report, quoted by both men, on 'The Situation in Catalonia', portions of which appeared in *The New Republic* on 2 December 1936 under the title 'On the Catalonian Front'. The complete text is reprinted in Galassi's selection of Cornford's writings.[32] In this report, Saville says, 'Cornford made abundantly clear his understanding and analysis of POUM', and he quotes it at length in order to refute 'Cunningham's political assessment of Cornford [which] rests entirely upon the supposed POUM-Cornford connection', stressing in particular the sentences with which his extract from Cornford's report begins:

POUM is a punishment for previous errors of the Communists and Socialists. The leaders are mostly Communist renegades (like Oranin) and ex-Trotskyists like Andrés Nin. Before 19th July it was as strong as the Communist Party, and its Trade Unions were stronger than the reformist UGT. But the sweep of the workers into all revolutionary organisations has meant that hundreds of revolutionary workers have swept also into the ranks of POUM. For instance, Grossi, the leader of the second column of POUM, an Oviedo miner under sentence of death at the time of the elections, though he may be both reckless and theatrical, is without question a sincere and courageous revolutionary with a mass following. But in spite of divisions in the leadership, the dominant policy is provocative and utterly dangerous. It is a parody of the Bolshevist tactics of 1917.... [Saville's ellipsis]

Fortunately, their influence is not growing dangerously. Their trade unions, a few months ago stronger than the UGT, have now very little influence, while the UGT grows in a geometrical progression. Their militia is the worst organised on the Aragon front; even brave and intelligent leaders like Grossi are incapable of giving their troops proper political, military, or organisational training. Thus their splitting policy is no longer a serious danger. They have little left beyond their sectarian political leaders: a well-produced newspaper, *La Batalla*, and two to three thousand of the worst-organised militia; brave enough, but incapable of a real sustained offensive through sheer inefficiency.[33]

As might be expected, Cunningham's reply stresses, contrariwise, Cornford's admiration, notwithstanding his reservations, for Grossi and for the genuine revolutionary motives of his 'mass following', which Saville had glossed over, and adds a jibe at political interference, in a note (omitted from Galassi's version) in the *New Republic* text of Cornford's essay by a notorious commissar of Party orthodoxy:

Nor does Saville mention the footnote that Pat Sloan, the Communist, Left Book Club author and Stalinising Russophile who edited *John Cornford: A Memoir*, added to Cornford's report on 'The Situation in Catalonia'. He added it in fact to the passage that Saville quotes, where Cornford is dismissing the political threat of the POUM despite the presence in it of such a magnetic leader as the miner Grossi, a 'sincere and courageous revolutionary' ('even brave and intelligent leaders like Grossi are incapable of giving their troops proper political, military, or organisational training'). Sloan's footnote interrupts such reflections sternly: 'The optimism of these remarks concerning the Anarchists and the POUM seem [sic] to be the only particular in which John Cornford's judgment erred. It was precisely the penetration of Fascists into these organizations – noted by J. C. – that made possible the Barcelona uprising of May 1937.'[34]

'Evidently', Cunningham concludes, 'what Saville calls Cornford's "understanding and analysis of POUM" was not sufficiently (in Saville's words) "abundantly clear" for the Party'.[35]

Sloan's intervention in fact provides the clue to the particular tone of Cornford's article. As Saville reveals, possibly for the first time, the article was originally a 'Political Report', 'in case the point has not been taken [...] written for the British CP and was read, among others, by Harry Pollitt, its general secretary [...] Pollitt certainly read the Political Report'.[36] Cornford, that is, was writing in the idiom of the Party, in a formal Report where Stalinist rhetoric was *de rigeur*, and no alternative interpretations of the historical realities to those of the current Party line would be acceptable. Thus he has to engage in the usual denigratory reference to Trotskyists and, in the passage just before Saville's excerpt, to POUM's 'provocative campaign for the arming of every man, woman and child in Barcelona for "the second revolution" at a time when all arms were wanted at the front'.[37] The overall context of such negative comments, however, is Cornford's clearly expressed approval of the Anarchist Durruti's response to the POUM campaign, in a telephone call which Durutti made to Barcelona, appealing 'for all Anarchist workers to send all sons to the front', together with Cornford's commendation, a couple of paragraphs earlier, of the 'magnificent responsibility and organising power of the [Anarchist] workers in their own Trade Unions, who are more and more adopting, though not yet consciously, the line of the Communists and Socialists, and will not permit wrecking tactics by their leaders'. There is of course a spirit of willed optimism and wishful special pleading to this last formulation, reinforced by the claim that, though 'they still refuse to take part in the official government' these Anarchists nevertheless 'gave their provisional support to the Government for the duration of the war'.[38]

By beginning his quotation from Cornford with the latter's ritual allusion to 'renegades' and 'ex-Trotskyists', Saville isolates this passage as if it were a specific and central indictment of POUM, when it is merely part of a reasoned and balanced analysis of all the elements in the Republican camp, starting with the 'bourgeois' coalition government headed by Companys and Casanovas and moving to a survey of the rest of the Spanish Left. Nowhere does Cornford indulge in the sectarian indictments and denunciations of treachery, subversion and 'objectively fascist' behaviour which characterised much Communist commentary on the other movements in the supposed 'united front' against fascism. He does indeed refer to the unsuccessful 'efforts of the semi-Trotskyist POUM (Partido Obrero d'Unificación Marxista) to break the People's Front', but adds at once that 'there has been no question of any serious political division'.[39] There is no indication that Cornford regards these as anything other than disagreements within the ranks of the genuine workers' movement, not acts of subversion and provocation by the 'Fifth Columnists' invoked by the Nationalist General Emilio Mola's 1936 broadcast to a besieged Madrid, a piece of psychological warfare eagerly taken advantage of by many within the Republic's ranks to settle old scores. On the contrary, in speaking of POUM as 'semi-Trotskyist', Cornford departs from Communist orthodoxy, which would recognise no such halfway house, and seems to allow scope for reconciliation and re-education, as in his wishful belief that the Anarchist workers are 'adopting, though not yet consciously' the PSUC line. Spelling out the initials of POUM, with all the emotional resonances attached to words like 'worker' and 'Marxist unity', might also have an incorporative polemic intent, while in speaking of Nin as an 'ex-Trotskyist', Cornford tries to hold the door open for a wider consensus than Party orthodoxy was prepared to tolerate. In similar vein, in a passage Saville omits between the two paragraphs he quotes, Cornford expands on what he means in writing of 'a parody of the Bolshevist tactics of 1917':

> The opposition to the People's Front and proposal instead to form a workers' bloc at the elections would have driven the Republicans into the arms of the reactionaries; it would have allowed the Lerroux Governments to continue in office: would have led the unarmed workers into struggle with the whole State machine. A further example of the pseudo-Bolshevism of POUM: Budyenny organised cavalry in the Russian revolution. So what must POUM do but organise cavalry too. They forgot that if Budyenny had had at his disposal roads in perfect working order and a fleet of fast lorries, he would not have organised cavalry but motorised columns instead.[40]

Possibly Cornford had not yet encountered the state of Spanish 'roads' (usually unmetalled tracks) away from the urban centres, particularly during winter rains. If he had, he might have been a little less dismissive of POUM policy on this matter. But his sarcasm here is certainly not an indictment of 'objectively counter-revolutionary' activity. On the contrary, in invoking 'Bolshevik' analogies from the heroic days of the Russian Revolution, he is quietly advising his orthodox Party readers that these people are genuine militants, whose errors may be comical but arise from an excess of revolutionary zeal, not from treachery. Nor is he convinced that the Party has always been right in the line it pursued. He is implicitly arguing for a wider tolerance and ecumenism in defining the forces of the Republic, and suggesting, too, that this is not only a moral precondition of revolutionary solidarity, but sound political strategy also, if the Party is to forge that 'welded front' without which the Republic will be defeated.

More interested in asserting Cornford's disapproval of POUM than in listening to what the man actually says, John Saville seems not to have noticed the astonishingly reckless departure from 'democratic centralist' norms in this twenty-year-old petty-bourgeois intellectual's rebuke to the unquestionable certainties of Party orthodoxy: 'POUM is a punishment for previous errors of the Communists and Socialists.' How dare this neophyte defector from the British bourgeoisie, still wet behind the ears, impute 'errors' to the infallible Party? Cornford's coded references to the Popular Front programme in his 'Report' are crucially significant in this context.

What the Seventh Congress Said

What is going on here is indicated most explicitly in the heretical hesitation, suppressed as uttered, in the fifth stanza of the published text of 'Full Moon at Tierz':

> All round the barren hills of Aragon
> Announce our testing has begun.
> Here what the Seventh Congress said,
> If true, if false, is live or dead,
> Speaks in the Oviedo mausers' tone.[41]

It's surprising that there has no been no critical consideration of these lines, particularly since, according to his biographers Peter Stansky and William Abrahams, they are, in their draft form, the first words Cornford wrote in his diary, and constitute the opening stanza of the diary version, only moved to the fifth stanza in the published version.[42] The words are, that is, the germ and stimulus of the whole poem, and indicate what was foremost in Cornford's mind as he confronted his first test in action with this POUM battalion. The next stanza of the poem, in the published version, opens up the specific significance of this allusion to the crucial Seventh Congress of the Communist International: 'Three years ago Dimitrov fought alone / And we stood taller when he won.'[43]

The reference, reinforced by the subsequent allusion to 'the Leipzig Dragon', is to Georgi Dimitrov, the Bulgarian Communist leader accused by the Nazis, in the Leipzig show trial in 1933, of setting fire to the Reichstag building, which event provided the pretext for Hitler's suspension of the

German constitution and his seizure of unconditional state power. Partly as a result of massive international publicity and pressure, Dimitrov was acquitted. Cornford's reference to him fighting alone is not quite accurate. His co-accused was the mentally unstable young Dutch anarchist and ex-Communist Marinus van der Lubbe, who was not so fortunate, being found guilty and subsequently beheaded by the Nazi state. Stephen Spender wrote a poem about van der Lubbe's manic laughter, manifest throughout the trial, and transmitted round the world by Movietone newsreel, while W.H. Auden also alluded to it in another, more famous poem.[44] Cornford's ignoring of Dimitrov's less successful co-defendant may be tactful silence in deference to the Party line: the Comintern was not interested in saving the life of a renegade ultra-leftist, whether innocent or not, and didn't want any competition to detract from its internationally celebrated triumph. Or it may be simply a matter of poetic expediency: it's important for the rhetoric of the poem that Dimitrov 'fought alone', so that lonely and isolated cadres like the poet himself can learn to stand taller in their solitude and, in the process, find a solidarity and shared identity ('Now with my Party, I stand quite alone').

But there is more to the Dimitrov reference than this, and it takes us right into the ambivalent heart of the poem. It was at the Seventh Congress of the Communist International in 1935 that Georgi Dimitrov, as its General Secretary, proposed, in a speech entitled 'The Unity of the Working Class against Fascism', a new strategy of anti-fascist collaboration with non-Communist organisations and movements. This strategy involved a major volte-face in Comintern policy, though it was not of course announced as such. Prior to this, the Comintern had espoused the so-called 'Third Period' strategy, which ran from 1928 until Hitler's seizure of power after 1933, and the growing threat of fascism throughout Europe, called for some substantial rethinking. 'What the Seventh Congress said', through the mouth of Dimitrov, was the call for the policy of a 'United Front against Fascism', more commonly known as the 'Popular Front'.

The ultra-leftist 'Third Period' strategy had affirmed that capitalism was now entering its third and final period, after its temporary stabilisation in the 1920s. National Communist parties had been required to denounce all other worker and socialist organisations as 'false lefts', and to reject collaboration with them and any participation in 'United Front' strategies. A cult of armed insurrection was advocated, irrespective of local circumstances, logistical capacity, or the likelihood of success. 'United front at the base', or 'from below', was contrasted with the allegedly 'revisionist' and 'opportunist' imposture of the 'united front from above', at the level of party leaderships. Unity 'from below' between all workers, irrespective of affiliation, required, in fact, that such workers respond to Communist initiatives so that, as a result of accepting 'informal' Communist leadership, they would sooner rather than later be 'won' to the Moscow line and subscribe formally to the leadership of the Comintern. The 'Popular Front' strategy, by contrast, went even further than advocating collaboration with the leadership of the previously reviled 'social fascist' parties. It now involved collaboration across classes with what was henceforth to be called the 'progressive bourgeoisie'. The French Communist leader, Maurice Thorez, whom Cornford invokes in the subsequent stanza of 'Full Moon at Tierz', was one of the architects of the Popular Front in France, having resisted overtures from the Socialists until 1934. While supporting from outside the Popular Front Government formed there after the 1936 elections, he kept the PCF out of direct participation in government, presumably on instructions from Moscow. He becomes, then, for Cornford, a figure of the disciplined cadre loyally implementing Party policy, irrespective of possible personal misgivings.

While the Popular Front policy was widely welcomed by liberal leftists such as Stephen Spender, many traditional Communists initially regarded the programme with distrust. Cornford's balancing formula, 'If true, if false, is live or dead', suggests that he shared these doubts, seeing resolution of the debate to lie in the outcome of armed conflict, 'the Oviedo mausers' tone'. Whether the Oviedo provenance of the POUM leader Grossi, singled out as a 'sincere and courageous revolutionary with a mass following' in his 'Political Report', unconsciously influenced Cornford's choice of this particular carbine rifle as the authoritative voice of the revolution, is now beyond speculation. But there is much evidence from his earlier writings that Cornford would, in the very recent past, have had considerable sympathy for the criticisms of Comintern policy (particularly in regard to the Popular Front) made by the Anarchists and 'semi-Trotskyists' among whom he was serving in Aragon, sentiments clearly shared, in fact, by those German ex-Communists of whom he writes with such admiration and affection in his letter to Heinemann.

In his essay 'What Communism Stands For' in *Christianity and the Social Revolution*, which was published in 1935, Cornford was convinced that the present era was 'the epoch of imperialist wars, of wars between the great powers for the redivision of the world', in which 'each successive crisis in the imperialist epoch is the prelude to a more desperate world war'.[45] For, he explained, 'the whole structure of capitalist rule eliminates the possibility of the peaceful conquest of power by the working class. If the working class ever wishes to take power, it must prepare for civil war.'[46] Indeed, he went further, in terms not often heard in the period of Popular Front politics, calling attention to 'The fate of the dozens of constitutional "socialist" Governments – in Germany, Austria, Australia, Great Britain, Scandinavia, Spain, etc., not one of which has been able to introduce an atom of lasting Socialism', which is 'the fate of the Socialists who "reject" civil war', and he continued with an attack on the policy of 'the left of the English Labour Party' for misunderstanding 'the whole structure of the capitalist State'.[47]

The writing of Cornford's essay probably predated the official formulation of the Popular Front policy, though by the time it was published that policy was in place. As a loyal Communist, he would have sought to accept the change in the Party line. Nevertheless, the essay shares the insurrectionary assumptions of Third Period strategy, and is clearly closer to the continuing criticisms of Popular Front strategy after 1935 by the non-Communist Left and by the Party's internal 'Left Opposition', not of course made public at the time. Such assumptions are even more apparent in the article 'Left?', which appeared in *Cambridge Left* in the winter of 1933–34. This essay asserts, in attacking Stephen Spender, that 'there is no middle position between revolution and reaction',[48] and actually quotes with approval two caustic stanzas from Auden's 'A Communist to Others', with the comment 'There is no ambiguity about this', commending that poem's 'far more virile and direct revolutionary form'.[49] Similarly, the essay 'The Struggle for Power in Western Europe', published in *Cambridge Left* in Spring 1934, shows little sign of a burgeoning Popular Front mentality, pouring scorn as it does on Social Democracy for facing 'in two directions – to show the bourgeoisie its absolute loyalty and to present the revolutionary workers revolutionary phrases without giving any lead in the immediate struggles'.[50] The tone as well as the tenor of all this corresponds closely to that subsequently to be found in Left critiques of the Popular Front policy. Indeed, quoting D.Z. Manuilsky's denunciation of the Second International at the CPSU's 17th Congress for seeking 'socialism but without the proletarian revolution', Cornford concluded that 'In sharp opposition to the theory and practice of the democratic transition from Capitalism to Socialism [of the Second International] stands the Communist International. It has always resolutely put forward the slogan of class against class'.[51] 'Class against class' was the precise formula of Third Period politics, rejected once the Popular Front was inaugurated. Cornford's private battle with his nerves, then, was also a struggle to convince himself that 'what the Seventh Congress said' was true, not false. If, as 'Full Moon at Tierz' reports, 'Communism was my waking time', it was for Cornford the Communism not of the Popular Front but of the Third Period strategy, now branded a sectarian ultra-leftist, 'Trotskyist' deviation. Cornford's perplexity, focused in the poem in that succinct antithesis, 'If true, if false', is apparent in the personal admission to Margot Heinemann early in his letter of 16–30 August:

> Now a bit about the political situation. That isn't easy to get straight, particularly as I haven't yet heard anyone explain the position of the Party

(and the militia here I am with are POUM – left sectarian semi-Trotskyists). But roughly this. The popular front tactics were worked magnificently to begin with. They won the elections. And under the slogan of the defence of the Republic, they enabled us to arm the workers when the Fascist revolt started. Up till then the position is quite clear. But now in Catalonia things are like this. There is a left Republican government. But, in fact, the real power is with the workers. There are 50,000 or more armed workers in Catalonia –and in the Barcelona patrols they are organised in the following proportions: 325 CNT (Anarchist), 185 ERC (left Republican). But this means simply the Civil Guard and the Guardia de Asalto, the police; 145 UGT (Soc.-Com.); 45 POUM. Thus the Anarchists predominate [...] The Anarchists appear to be preparing to attack the Government after the fall of Saragossa. That would be disastrous. The only possible tactics for the Party are to place themselves at the head of the movement, get it under control, force recognition from the Government of the social gains of the revolution, and prevent at all costs an attack on the Government – unless the Government actually begins to sabotage the fight against Fascism. That may be what the Party is doing. But I have a fear that it is a little too mechanical in its application of People's Front tactics. It is still concentrating too much on trying to neutralise the petty bourgeoisie – when by far the most urgent task is to win the anarchist workers, which is a special technique and very different from broad Seventh Congress phrases. But I don't really know.[52]

In Barcelona, he continues, 'one can understand physically what the dictatorship of the proletariat means', adding, a little later, 'It is genuinely a dictatorship of the majority, supported by the overwhelming majority'.[53] The description of POUM as 'left sectarian semi-Trotskyists' is orthodox enough, though that 'semi-' again adds a cautionary note, but there is no indication that he regards them as untrustworthy comrades to fight alongside. This is all the more significant in that, exactly contemporaneously, the first of Stalin's 'show trials', of the 'Trotskyite-Zinovievite Terrorist Centre', was being conducted in Moscow in the week of 19–24 August, though it is unclear whether Cornford was aware of this, given the Republic's strict censorship of external and internal news.

The ostensible loyalty of the disciplined cadre to Party policy on the Popular Front seems more formal than real here. Significantly, he twice speaks of the policy as mere 'tactics', in a context where the duality of 'tactics' and 'strategy' was part of everyday discourse. The main purpose of such 'tactics' is perceived as winning the election and ensuring the arming of the workers 'under the slogan of the defence of the Republic'. Note that he doesn't say the popular front tactics 'worked', but (unless this is an error of writing or transcription) that, with a machiavellian twist, they 'were worked'. Behind the formula 'a little too mechanical' lies, I would suggest, a deeper unhappiness with the Party line. This becomes sharper in the light of that clearly 'Third Period' emphasis on the priority of having an armed working class with 'real power' rising from below. Cornford does not here see an armed, largely Anarchist-oriented working class as a threat to the cause, but rather as the precondition of its survival. Though, as Cornford writes, 'The Anarchists appear to be preparing to attack the Government', he does not propose their suppression. Instead, in terms clearly derived from the Third Period strategy of 'unity from below', he urges the need for the Party to place itself 'at the head of the movement'. This would not only protect the 'left Republican government' (unless it 'actually begins to sabotage the fight against Fascism', in which case it would not deserve protection) but also 'force recognition from the Government of the social gains of the revolution'. In short it would preserve 'the dictatorship of the proletariat'. This is very far, of course, from the actual trajectory taken by the Spanish Communists and their Soviet mentors in the months that followed.[54] On the contrary, the Communist line was to continue to concentrate 'on trying to neutralise the petty bourgeoisie', that is, in effect, to placate that class, at the expense of what Cornford believed to be 'the most urgent task [...] to win the anarchist workers'. Whatever (in Communist parlance) the 'correct line' was in these circumstances, Cornford's scepticism about the theoretical, 'textbook' nature of the policy's implementation, and his countervailing insistence on the real complexity of class and political interests and opportunities on the ground, not only derive from his Third Period predispositions, but are hardly distinguishable from the kind of critique George Orwell offered of Communist policy in Catalonia a year later, after the suppression of POUM and other Left forces in May 1937. Cornford's implicit and, for such a loyal cadre, somewhat astounding dismissal of Party orthodoxy, in that contemptuous reference to 'broad Seventh Congress phrases', full of the activist's contempt for theorising dogmatism, feeds right into the moment of stumbling and prevarication which provided the initial impulse for 'Full Moon at Tierz': 'Here what the Seventh Congress said, / If true, if false, is live or dead', to be proven only by hard practical reality, the praxis of 'the Oviedo mausers' tone', and a will hard as the metal of his gun.

Far from being a Communist hack then (something on which at times Cunningham and Saville appear almost to be agreed), Cornford, struggling to conform to Party doctrine while holding on to his fundamental commitment to an insurrectionist, Third Period agenda, seems to be trying to imagine a strategy that would reconcile, in his own word, 'weld', defence of the Republic with the cause of proletarian revolution, of which the Spanish War, and his own life, were in his perception only single, isolated moments. It is in this light that we must read his tribute, in the closing paragraph of his letter to Heinemann, to the integrity and authenticity of his German comrades, men, he had already told her, who 'genuinely believe the C.I. has deserted the revolution', but who remain 'the finest people in some ways I've ever met', and who gave him back a conviction of his own identity as a principled fighter for the world revolution, 'For Communism *and* for liberty' (my emphasis):

> Since meeting the Germans I feel like myself again, no longer lost, and revolutionary again. Before I was too lost to feel anything but lost. Now I'll fight like hell and I think I'll enjoy it. They are the finest people in some ways I've ever met. In a way they have lost everything, have been through enough to break most people, and remain strong and cheerful and humorous. If anything is revolutionary it is these comrades.[55]

What emerges from 'Full Moon at Tierz', then, is the strain of such an internal struggle. But what that struggle witnesses to is the integrity and dignity of Cornford's commitment to Spain, and to the wider anti-fascist cause, which for him were inseparable from the international proletarian revolution, a cause for which he was prepared, in Auden's phrase, to present his life.

Notes

1. This essay extends and in places reprises an argument first developed in my chapter, 'From "Class Against Class" to the Hitler-Stalin Pact: Some Reflections on the Unwavering Line', in Jennifer Birkett and Stan Smith, eds, *Right/Left/Right: Revolving Commitments, France and Britain 1929–1950* (Newcastle: Cambridge Scholars Publishing, 2008), pp. 7–28. See also Birkett and Smith (eds), *Revolving Commitment: France and Britain 1929–1950*, a Special Issue of the e-journal *E-REA: revue d'études Anglophones* 4.1 (Autumn 2007): pp. 3–16.
2. W.H Auden, *Spain* (London: Faber and Faber, 1937), p. 10.
3. John Lehmann and Stephen Spender, eds, *Poems for Spain* (London: Gollancz, 1939).
4. John Lehmann, *The Whispering Gallery* (London: Longmans, Green, 1955), p. 273.
5. Lehmann, *Whispering Gallery*, p. 332.
6. Christopher Isherwood, *Lions and Shadows: An Education in the Twenties* (1938; London: Methuen, 1979), p. 46.
7. The concept of 'the test' was not restricted to members of the intellectual elite such as Isherwood and Lehmann, but had a more general currency. Janet Murray, for example, 'Chairman of the Edinburgh and District Joint Committee for Spanish Relief', wrote to her husband Tom, an International Brigader, just before he took part in the crossing of the Ebro in July 1938, that 'You are now having the test you talked of. I know that you will be acquitting yourself with credit' (quoted in Daniel Gray, *Homage to Caledonia: Scotland and the Spanish Civil War* [Edinburgh: Luath Press, 2008], pp. 120–21). The Ebro battle turned out to be the Republic's last major victory, though at the time it looked like the prelude to the final defeat of the Nationalists.

8 Stephen Spender, 'Diary', *London Review of Books* (9 April 1992), p. 25.
9 Stephen Spender, *World Within World* (London: Hamish Hamilton, 1951), p. 311.
10 W.H Auden, 'Authority in America', *Griffin* (4 March 1955), p. 9.
11 Anon. [Hugh l'Anson Fausset], 'Left Wing Poets and Spain', *Times Literary Supplement* (4 March 1939), p. 131.
12 [Fausset], p. 131.
13 [Fausset], p. 131.
14 Jonathan Galassi (ed.), *Understand the Weapon Understand the Wound: Selected Writings of John Cornford* (Manchester: Carcanet New Press, 1976), pp. 38–40.
15 Galassi, p. 39.
16 Galassi, pp. 171–81.
17 Galassi, p. 180.
18 Galassi, p. 180.
19 Galassi, p. 180.
20 Galassi, p. 39.
21 Galassi, p. 39.
22 Galassi, p. 40.
23 Galassi, p. 38.
24 Galassi, p. 40.
25 Galassi, p. 39.
26 Galassi, p. 40.
27 Galassi, pp. 38–40 passim.
28 Galassi, p. 39.
29 John Saville, 'Valentine Cunningham and the Poetry of the Spanish Civil War', *Socialist Register* 18 (1981), pp. 270–84; Valentine Cunningham, 'Saville's Row with the *Penguin Book of Spanish Civil War Verse*', *Socialist Register* 19 (1982), pp. 269–83.
30 Valentine Cunningham, ed., *The Penguin Book of Spanish Civil War Verse* (Harmondsworth: Penguin Books, 1980).
31 Saville, p. 279. Pollitt was indeed far from being a simple Stalinist hack, to the extent that at the time of the Nazi-Soviet pact he was sacked from the position of General Secretary of the CPGB by its central committee, since he was unable to endorse the official party line. He was only restored to leadership when Hitler's invasion of the Soviet Union in June 1941 instantly converted what had previously been designated an inter-imperialist conflict into a war of proletarian patriotism.
32 Galassi, pp. 108–25.
33 Saville, p. 274; Galassi, pp. 112–13.
34 Cunningham, *Socialist Register*, p. 279.
35 Cunningham, *Socialist Register*, p. 279.
36 Saville, p. 274.
37 Galassi, p. 111.
38 Galassi, p. 111.
39 Galassi, pp. 109–11 passim.
40 Galassi, p. 112.
41 Galassi, p. 38
42 Peter Stansky and William Abrahams, *Journey to the Frontier: Two Roads to the Spanish Civil War* (London: Constable, 1966), p. 347.
43 Galassi, p. 38.
44 Stephen Spender, 'Van der Lubbe', *Poems* (London: Faber and Faber, 1933, 2nd edition 1934), pp. 39–40; W.H. Auden, poem XXI, *Look, Stranger!* (London: Faber and Faber, 1936), pp. 50–52 (p. 51).

45 John Cornford, 'What Communism Stands For', in John Lewis, ed., *Christianity and the Social Revolution* (London: Gollancz, 1935), p. 242.
46 Lewis, p. 256.
47 Lewis, p. 257.
48 Galassi, p. 59.
49 Galassi, p. 61.
50 Galassi, p. 66.
51 Galassi, pp. 66–7. Although Manuilsky, a leading Comintern theoretician, author in 1932 of *Social Democracy – Stepping-stone to Fascism:* [...] *Address Delivered to the Executive Committee of the Communist International* (London: Modern Books, 1932), publicly endorsed the 'Popular Front' turn announced by Dimitrov at the 7th Congress , he continued to express reservations in private. According to Igor Lukes, off the platform, 'Manuilsky criticized the view that fighting Nazism meant not fighting capitalism, and he reaffirmed the theory (he called it "Stalin's theory") that Nazism and social democracy were "not antipodes but twins."' Rather, the Popular Front against Hitler was 'a means to accelerate the civil conflicts latent within capitalism in order to bring about the revolution the communists could not provoke on their own' (Igor Lukes, *Czechoslovakia between Stalin and Hitler: The Diplomacy of Edvard Benes in the 1930s* [Oxford: Oxford University Press, 1996], p. 73).
52 Galassi, p. 173.
53 Galassi, p. 174.
54 The most balanced and scrupulously impartial narrative of these times is that provided by Paul Preston, *The Spanish Civil War: Reaction, Revolution and Revenge* (London: Harper Perennial, 2006).
55 Galassi, p. 181.

Reviews

Stanley Aronowitz, *Against Schooling: For an Education that Matters*. Boulder, CO: Paradigm Books, 2008, xix + 196 pp. $80; £24.95. ISBN: 978-1-59451-502-6.

This book is one of several (though more vigorous in its mode of delivery) which point to the growing divergence between 'schooling' and 'education'. Of course, that divergence is not generally recognised. The two words are often used interchangeably. And so, as the book so effectively illustrates, the concept of 'education' becomes impoverished, losing the evaluative significance with which it is properly associated. The 'educated person' becomes no more and no less than the 'well-schooled person' – the one who has helped the school to hit its targets, to meet its performance indicators, to convince the auditors and to satisfy its customers. The 'high stakes testing regime', which now dominates both sides of the Atlantic, causes teachers to teach to the test, and to see success in the proportion of learners who pass these tests with specific grades. In England, certainly, there is the consequent growth of league tables through which some schools win parental support in 'the market place', whilst others (often those serving the most disadvantaged areas) get stigmatised as 'failing schools'.

Consequently, the teacher is now expected 'to deliver the curriculum' – a curriculum determined elsewhere and one which has to be delivered if targets are to be met. The raising of standards is but a 'euphemism for the subordination of pedagogy to tests' and the growth of 'credentialism'. Hence, as Aronowitz says in his introduction,

> Whether intentioned or not, having denied the value of creative pedagogy and teacher classroom autonomy, the effect of *No Child Left Behind* and its local variants has been to introduce the teacherless curriculum in which there is no room for interpretation and creativity.

This general message, as well as being well researched and justified philosophically, is illuminated in the book by way of Aronowitz's personal and family narratives – the Jewish immigrant family in the Bronx, early family membership of the International Ladies' Garment Workers' Union, working-class with a lust for knowledge (literature, politics and social analysis): 'I came from a family of unschooled but highly educated members of the "labour aristocracy".'

Aronowitz's disillusion with schooling but inherited passion for education resulted in the establishment of alternative schools, following in a long tradition of those similarly disillusioned with traditional schooling – Dewey, Freire, Illich, Gramsci, Meier and many others (though Dewey is criticised for not seeing the significance of social class in his conception of education as an enrichment and as an engagement in democracy). The confusion of 'schooling' with 'education' is seen to affect particularly the most disadvantaged groups, denied, in their more 'useful' or vocational curricula, that access to our cultural heritage which would empower them to see the world differently and to give them the tools to change it. Equal access to schooling does not give equal access to education, for 'education' must be broader than schooling. It 'may be defined as the collective and individual reflection on the totality of life experience: what we learn from peers, parents and the socially situated culture of which they are a part'. Schooling, to be truly educational, must be an extension of, and reflection upon, those deep felt experiences – a deepening and critical understanding of them, a making sense through the cultural tools ('the collective reflection') we have inherited. The philosopher Michael Oakeshott does not get a mention, but his metaphor of education as being an introduction to 'the conversation between the generations of mankind' through which we come to appreciate the voice of poetry, the voice of science, the voice of philosophy, would, I am sure, meet with Aronowitz's approval. Certainly it would do so with the earlier generations of his family for whom there was a clear connection between their lives and the search for knowledge through which those lives, individually and collectively, could be improved.

That failure to connect 'schooling' with experience is reflected particularly in the neglect of 'popular culture' (music, art and social activities) which shapes young people's consciousness and behaviour – thereby 'denying the validity of student experiences'. But, argues Aronowitz, this connection of education with the more intelligent and critical understanding of experience requires a more democratic framework, through which education in its different forms (not just in reformed schooling) is located in different local 'sites', including those of employment, where there is a need for broader understanding and critical thinking. Schooling should be seen as but one aspect of life-long learning.

This has many implications: first, undermining the dominance of central bureaucracies' dictation of what are to count as 'standards'; second, the elimination of testing regimes which are supposed to reflect those standards; third, the education of teachers such that, intellectually equipped, they can draw upon the intellectual and cultural traditions we have inherited in order to illuminate those experiences; fourth, empowering local groups and societies to ensure that there is this more creative educational response to their interests, needs and aspirations.

This is an important book – radical in its analysis and proposed ways forward. It comes at an important time, when there is growing disillusion with the narrow understanding of education as it is embodied in schools shaped by the 'performance management' and centralisation instituted by dominant governments. We need to be reminded, as Aronowitz reminds us, of a different vision, one that is rooted in a different understanding of human development and social improvement.

Richard Pring
Oxford University

Barbara Hardy, *Dickens and Creativity*. London: Continuum, 2008. xvi + 181 pp. £66 hb, ISBN 978-1847-64592; £19.99 pb, ISBN 978-1-84706-459-2

Soon after Dickens began work on *Dombey and Son*, he told a friend that he had given up reading Crabbe. He used to like him, he said, but now found the poet dreary and lacking in imagination. In reaching this conclusion, he could have been echoing Wordsworth and Hazlitt, both of whom had whacked Byron's 'Pope in worsted stockings' for his undue attention to 'mere matters of fact'. But my guess is that Dickens was covering his tracks. He must have realised that anyone who had read 'Procrastination', one of the *Tales in Verse* (1812), and who was keeping up with the serialisation of *Dombey*, would be bound to notice the debt owed to Crabbe for the description in chapter 5 of Dombey's library. Nor was this by any means the first time Dickens had plundered the poet's work. The episode of 'Peter Grimes' in *The Borough* (1810), is without doubt a, if not *the*, starting point for the description of those paranoid fears that prey on Sikes's mind after he has killed Nancy. And some twenty-five years later, when he writes about Orlick, the lonely, brutish murderer of the marsh in *Great Expectations*, Dickens is evidently still remembering Grimes's enforced isolation on the mud-banks, 'Where all, presented to the eye or ear, / Oppressed the soul with misery, grief, and fear.'

Dickens's desire to disguise his debt isn't, I think, to be explained as embarrassment – even guilt – at his borrowings. After all, he more than repays them. It has more to do with a perhaps not fully conscious wish to be thought of as that newish type of writer, the natural genius. There was a precedent for this. In the famous Introduction to what became known as the Kilmarnock edition of his *Poems, 1786*, Robert Burns insists that he works purely from inspiration. He does not, so he says, 'look down for a rural theme, with an eye to Theocritus and Virgil [...] Unacquainted with the necessary requisites for commencing Poet by rule, he sings the sentiments and manners he felt and saw in himself and his rustic compeers.' Burns, who had in fact read much, was deliberately marketing himself as a peasant poet. In his edition of Burns's Life and Letters, Chambers records that whenever someone pointed out to the poet a borrowing or allusion or half-quotation from another poet, Burns would not allow it, especially if he felt it might prevent the sale of a single copy of his poems.

In the introduction to *Dickens and Creativity*, and elsewhere in the book, Barbara Hardy says that Dickens was 'a writer not widely or deeply read. Not conventionally educated in the classics like Thackeray, or self-educated in many subjects and languages like George Eliot'. Perhaps, although I have to say that I have always thought reports of Dickens's lack of reading are greatly exaggerated. He may on occasions have presented himself as a man of no learning, but the truth is otherwise. G.H. Lewes was shocked at the few books in the Inimitable's library. I suspect that it suited Dickens to be written off as a philistine by the *Westminster Review* set. After all, they didn't take novels seriously. Novels weren't art. But, given his astonishingly adhesive memory, one small head could carry all he knew. And what he knew, some of it derived from long hours of reading in the British Museum reading room, included French and Italian as well as a fair amount of Latin, and familiarity with books that, as his biographer John Forster attested, took him a long way from (and past) that of the 'conventionally educated'. I think it was A.D. Lindsay who recalled an occasion when he was invited to talk to a group of Welsh miners about nineteenth-century philosophy. He arrived prepared to share his views on, among others, Hegel and his idealist followers such as T.H. Green and F.H. Bradley, and found that the miners wanted to talk about, among others, Max Stirner and Herbert Spencer, whose writings they knew intimately and about whom Lindsay himself knew very little.

And saying this leads me to want to lay bare what I hope is a friendly disagreement with Hardy. Because the fact that Dickens didn't go to university and wasn't conventionally well-read does not mean that he wasn't well-read in ways which, though they lie outside the confines of orthodoxy, nevertheless fed his extraordinary creative powers. Many of the great writers of the past two hundred years, perhaps the majority, were without conventional education, if by that we mean attendance at an Oxbridge college. I doubt that Crabbe was much read in the long stretch of the nineteenth century, although Dickens did read him. (As did most novelists: he was the novelists' poet.) Hardy has nothing to say about Crabbe. Nor does she mention Blake. But how can you read *Bleak House* and not see Blake's importance to Dickens's vision of the great and dirty city of London where his novel is set? As with Crabbe, Blake wasn't much read in the middle years of the nineteenth century. Certainly, the conventionally educated barely knew of his existence. But Carlyle knew all right, and Carlyle was Dickens's friend. And the anthology of poems about chimney sweeps put together in 1827 by James Montgomery, friend of Wordsworth, included Blake's two Songs; and Montgomery knew R.H. Horne, who was part of the circle of radicals in which Dickens moved in the 1830s and 1840s; and Horne, author of fiery plays and the 'farthing' epic, *Orion*, became a regular contributor to *Household Words*. Then there is Wordsworth, the lost leader. Hardy's references to him are routine. Yet Wordsworth plainly influences moments in *Oliver Twist* and, crucially, *David Copperfield*.

Perhaps few of the conventionally educated in the middle years of the nineteenth century read much of Fielding, Sterne or Smollett. Hardy barely mentions the first two and has nothing to say about the third. But consider titles alone: *Tom Jones, Tristram Shandy, Peregrine Pickle, Nicholas Nickleby, Martin Chuzzlewit*, let alone Dickens's use of the picaresque. Moreover, Dickens from the first is a great parodist and satirist. Yes, we all know that *Oliver Twist* revisits 'Newgate Novels', as well as echoing Bunyan. But Bunyan isn't mentioned by Hardy, anymore than is the King James Bible, though both massively influenced Dickens's prose, its rhythms as well as its different rhetorical and dramatic postures. And to understand *Nicholas Nickleby* it helps to know something of the 'Silver-Fork' novels of that period. With the exception of the Bible, all these lie outside the bounds of what is expected of the conventionally educated, but for literally thousands of others, including Dickens, these were all common reading, and they provided points of reference he could creatively direct his own writing at and from.

Hardy has a good chapter on Dickens's engagement with Shakespeare, whose plays he seems to have known by heart. But she misses the all-important fact that Dickens re-read the entire corpus when Macready lent him his edition for the journey to America in 1842, and that *Martin Chuzzlewitt*, the novel which comes out of that experience, not only takes a newly intense delight in English idiom (of a kind that Shakespeare first fully tries out in the *Henry IV* diptych) but that Mrs Gamp is surely Dickens's version of Falstaff. Here, creativity is in part a reaction against the new world, focused by Dickens's reading of and thinking about Shakespeare.

As to 'The Awareness of Art', which is the title of one of her chapters: Hardy has interesting things to say about Dickens's powers of observation, but nothing at all about the ways he and Browne at their best worked together to create a complementarity of word and visual image that allows us essential insights into a novel's characters and their full meanings. To take one example: when towards the end of *Dombey and Son* Edith Skewton and Carker run away to France, 'Phiz' provides an illustration that shows the pair in a hotel bedroom. Carker sits, legs apart, scowling but defeated as Edith, who is standing, denounces him; her gesture alone makes clear that she isn't about to become his mistress. That he should be sitting in her presence marks the social indecorum of the occasion. But more important, her extended arm is pointed, sword-like, at his crotch. Above her head, on the bedroom wall, hangs a painting of Judith with the head of Holofernes. Few could have seen such an image in the middle years of the nineteenth century, and indeed it is pretty remarkable that Phiz alludes to it. (It isn't in the written text.) But no doubt trusting to his readers' knowledge of the Apocrypha, if not of Artemisia Gentileschi, he does. Not only that. On a table behind Edith stands a small statuette of a mounted Amazon in the act of hurling a spear. Now that *could* have been seen by plenty of people, because one just like it was cast in Berlin in 1847, and, four years later, it was to be on show at the Great Exhibition. Hogarth was the first great artist to use pictures within pictures as a way of commenting on the main action (Rapes of the Gods above the Rake's Progress) and in this he was followed by his great admirers, Rowlandson and Gillray. They incorporated references to daily trivia and phenomena that would have been familiar to their thousands of viewers, who for the most part stared at the work through shop windows. Phiz does the same. Hence the Amazon on horseback. How do I know this? From trawling through the pages of the *Art Journal*, as thousands then did. It's from the *Art Journal* and such catalogues as Loudon's *Cottage, Farm, and Villa Architecture* (1839) that you can find how Dickens and Browne used their creative genius – I think Browne deserves the epithet – in order to create visual and verbal texts that could be read by their contemporaries in a manner, and with an understanding, to which our divisions of art into high and low blinds us.

None of this is to take away from the many good things to be found in *Dickens and Creativity*. In addition to the chapter on Shakespeare there's a lively discussion on 'Talkative Men and Women' and, perhaps less original but nevertheless fruitful, a helpful account of 'Forecast and Fantasy in *Little Dorrit*'. I remember as an undergraduate plodding through Geoffrey Bullough's three volume *Narrative and Dramatic Sources of Shakespeare's Plays*, and, when I finished, deciding that I'd learnt virtually nothing about what makes Shakespeare a great dramatist. Barbara Hardy's book undoubtedly does point to some of the ways in which Dickens's creative genius works and identifies a number of the sources from which it comes. But …. But …. *But* ….

John Lucas
Nottingham Trent University

Raymond Williams Foundation (RWF)

Formerly the Raymond Williams Memorial Fund, the RWF has among its aims 'to commemorate the works of Raymond Williams, in particular in the sphere of adult education for the benefit of the public'.

The 21st annual Raymond Williams weekend took place in May with *Keywords* as its theme. Sessions were led by Dai Smith, Mark Fisher, Catherine Belsey and Erica Brook.

The 22nd weekend will be held at the Wedgwood Memorial College (WMC) on 7–9 May 2010. The theme will be *Towards 2020* (loosely based on Williams's book *Towards 2000*).

In August 2009, RWF received confirmation that its bid for nearly £10k from the *Learning Revolution – Transformation Fund* had been successful. The Fund is administered by the National Institute for Adult and Continuing Education.

This will enable the development of the North Staffordshire Pubs project, whereby discussion groups focus upon social, political, philosophical and international affairs in the context of citizenship education. This additional funding will also enable a related a residential school to be held at the WMC plus several Workers Educational Association residential and day schools.

We continue to gain members, but not many. We know that it will not be easy for us to gain an extended membership during an economic crisis which has already had a negative impact on charities generally. We have, however, done better than expected with our life-memberships. So, we are viable, always welcoming new members and donations.

Derek Tatton
RWF Administrator and RWS Executive Committee Member
www.raymondwilliamsfoundation.org.uk

Call for Papers

Special Issue: *The Long Revolution* **Revisited**

To celebrate the fiftieth anniversary of Raymond Williams's *The Long Revolution* in 1961, *Key Words* is planning a special issue to discuss the book and its themes including their contemporary relevance. In particular we would welcome submissions on such topics as Williams's discussion of the creative mind, the analysis of culture, individuals and societies and images of society; the subject matter of Part Two of the book, including education and British society, the reading public, the popular press, Standard English, the social history of British writers and of dramatic forms; and the analysis of 'Britain in the 1960s' that comprises Part Three.

In the first instance, proposals for papers should be sent before 31 March 2010 to Dr Catherine Clay at catherine.clay@ntu.ac.uk or School of Arts and Humanities, Nottingham Trent University, Clifton Campus, Nottingham NG11 8NS, United Kingdom.

Style Notes for Contributors

Presentation of Copy
Key Words is an internationally refereed academic journal. In the first instance typescripts for prospective publication should be submitted to the Contributions Editor (details may be found on the inside back cover). Articles should normally be no longer than 6,000 words; reviews should typically be between 1,500 and 2,000 words. Articles should be double spaced, with generous margins, and pages should be numbered consecutively. For matters of style not addressed below, please refer to *The Chicago Manual of Style*, 15th edn or http://www.chicagomanualofstyle.org/contents.html. Contributors who fail to observe these notes may be asked to revise their submission in accordance with them.

Provision of Text in Electronic Format
Key Words is prepared electronically. Consequently, contributors whose work is accepted for publication will be asked to supply a file copy of their work (either on disc, CD-ROM or by electronic mail) to the Contributions Editor. The preferred word processing format is Microsoft Word (any version).

References and Bibliographic Conventions
Citations in *Key Words* appear as endnotes at the conclusion of each contribution. Essays presented for prospective publication should adopt this style. Endnote markers should be given in arabic numerals and positioned after, not before, punctuation marks, e.g. '.¹' rather than '¹.'. With no bibliography, full details must be given in a note at the first mention of any work cited. Subsequent citations can then use the short form or a cross-reference. Headline-style capitalisation is used. In headline style, the first and last words of title and subtitle and all other major words are capitalised. Titles of books and journals should be formatted in italics (not underlined).

Please cite books in the following manner:

On first citation: Raymond Williams and Michael Orrom, *Preface to Film* (London: Film Drama, 1954).

On subsequent citations: Williams and Orrom, *Preface to Film*, 12.

Style Notes for Contributors

Please cite journal articles in the following manner:

Patrick Parrinder, 'Politics, Letters and the National Curriculum', *Changing English* 2, no. 1 (1994): 29.

Chapters in books should be referenced in the following way:

Andrew McRae, 'The Peripatetic Muse: Internal Travel and the Cultural Production of Space in Pre-Revolutionary England', in *The Country and the City Revisited: England and the Politics of Culture, 1550–1850*, ed. Gerald MacLean, Donna Landry, and Joseph P. Ward (Cambridge: Cambridge University Press, 1999), 41–57.

For internet articles:

Raymond Williams Society Executive, 'About the Raymond Williams Society', Raymond Williams Society, http://www.raymondwilliams.co.uk/ (accessed 26 March 2009).

Please refer to newspaper articles in the following way:

John Mullan, 'Rebel in a Tweed Suit', *The Observer*, 28 May 2005, Features and Reviews section, 37.

A thesis should be referenced in the following manner:

E. Allen, 'The Dislocated Mind: The Fictions of Raymond Williams' (PhD diss., Liverpool John Moores University, 2007), 22–9.

Conference papers should be cited in the following style:

Dai Smith, 'Translating Raymond Williams' (paper presented at the Raymond Williams's Culture and Society@50 conference, Canolfan Dylan Thomas Centre, Swansea, 7 November 2008).

Quotations

For quotations use single quotation marks, and double quotation marks for quotations within quotations. Punctuation is used outside quotations.. Ensure that all spellings, punctuation, abbreviations etc. within a quotation are rendered exactly as in the original, including errors, which should be signalled by the authorial interpolation '(*sic*)'.

Books Received

Book reviews should open with full bibliographic details of the text under review. These details should include (in the following order): in bold type, first name(s) and surname(s) of author(s), or first name(s) and surname(s) of editor(s) followed by a parenthetic '(ed.)' or '(eds); in italics, the full title of the volume followed by a period and a hard return; then, in regular type, the place of publication, publisher and date of publication; the page extent of the volume, including front papers numbered in Roman numerals; the price (where available) of the supplied copy and an indication of 'pb.' or 'hb.'; and the ISBN of the supplied copy. For example:

Dai Smith, *Raymond Williams: A Warriors Tale.*
Parthian Books, 2008. xviii + 514 pp. £24.99 hb. ISBN 978 1 905762 56 9.

Revised with effect from Volume 8.